THE CLONE WARS

THE SMUGGLER'S CODE

DESIGNER **KRYSTAL HENNES**

ASSISTANT EDITOR **FREDDYE LINS**

EDITOR **DAVE MARSHALL**

PUBLISHER **MIKE RICHARDSON**

Special thanks to Joanne Chan Taylor, Leland Chee, Troy Alders, Carol Roeder, Jann Moorhead, and David Anderman at Lucas Licensing.

Published by Dark Horse Books, a division of Dark Horse Comics, Inc.
10956 SE Main Street, Milwaukie, OR 97222

DarkHorse.com | StarWars.com

International licensing: 503.905.2377
To find a comics shop in your area, call the Comic Shop Locator Service toll-free at 1.888.266.4226
First edition: June 2013 | ISBN 978-1-61655-108-7

10 9 8 7 6 5 4 3 2 1

Printed in China

Library of Congress Cataloging-in-Publication Data

Aclin, Justin.
 The smuggler's code / script, Justin Aclin ; art, Eduardo Ferrara ; colors, Michael Atiyeh ; lettering, Michael Heisler ; cover art, Bengal. – First edition.
     pages cm. – (Star Wars, the clone wars)
 Summary: "Jedi Obi-Wan Kenobi strikes out to bring in a fugitive on his own; he earns a favor from a local smuggler who may be more trouble for Obi-Wan than his help is actually worth"–Provided by publisher.
 ISBN 978-1-61655-108-7
 1. Graphic novels. I. Ferrara, Eduardo, 1968- illustrator. II. Bengal, 1976- illustrator. III. Title.
 PZ7.7.A28Smu 2013
 741.5'973–dc23
                          2013000694

THE CLONE WARS

THE SMUGGLER'S CODE

SCRIPT **JUSTIN ACLIN**

ART **EDUARDO FERRARA**

COLORS **MICHAEL ATIYEH**

LETTERING **MICHAEL HEISLER**

COVER ART **BENGAL**

DARK HORSE BOOKS

LUCAS BOOKS

This story takes place sometime during season 4 of *The Clone Wars*.

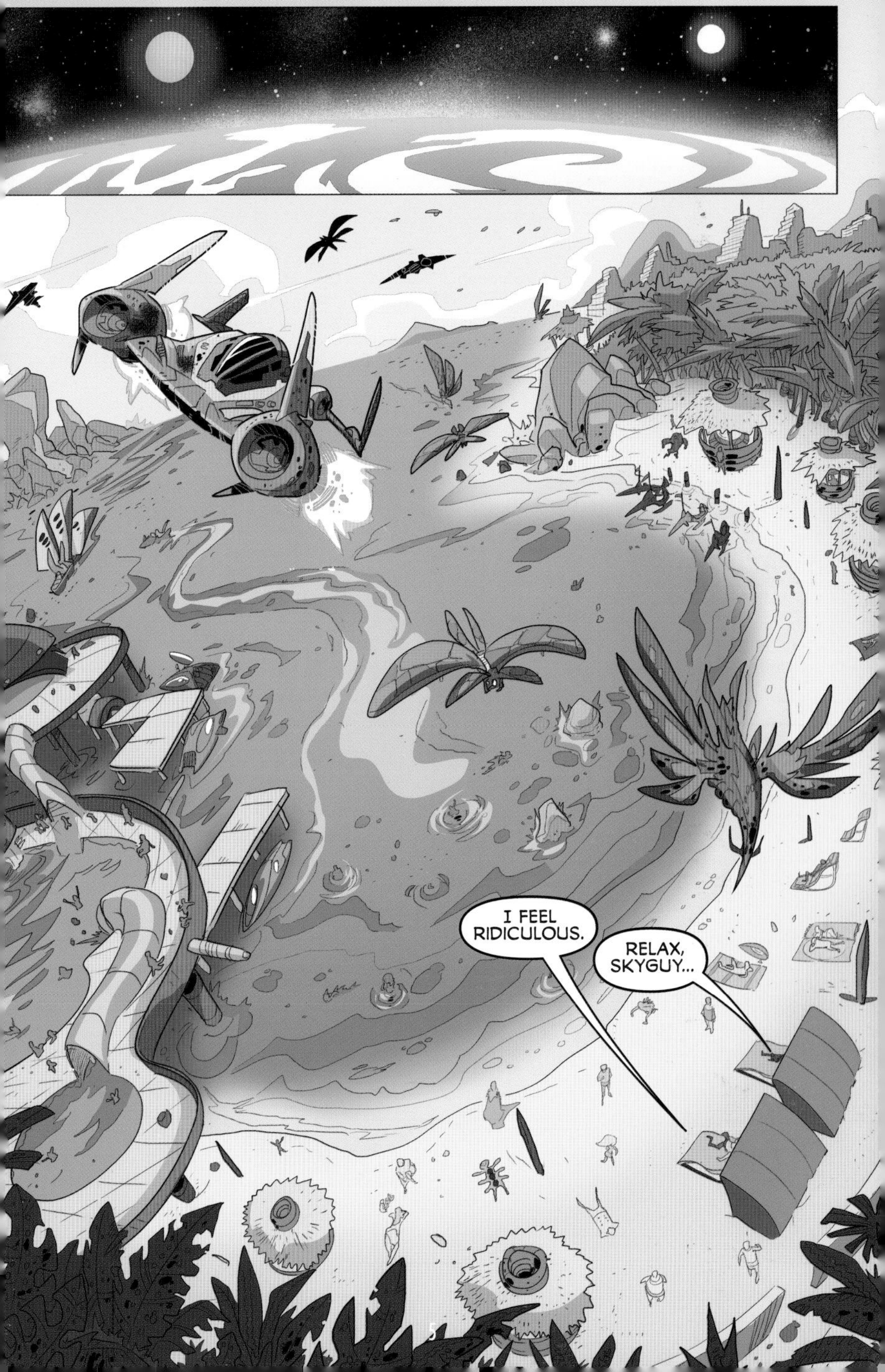
I FEEL RIDICULOUS.
RELAX, SKYGUY...

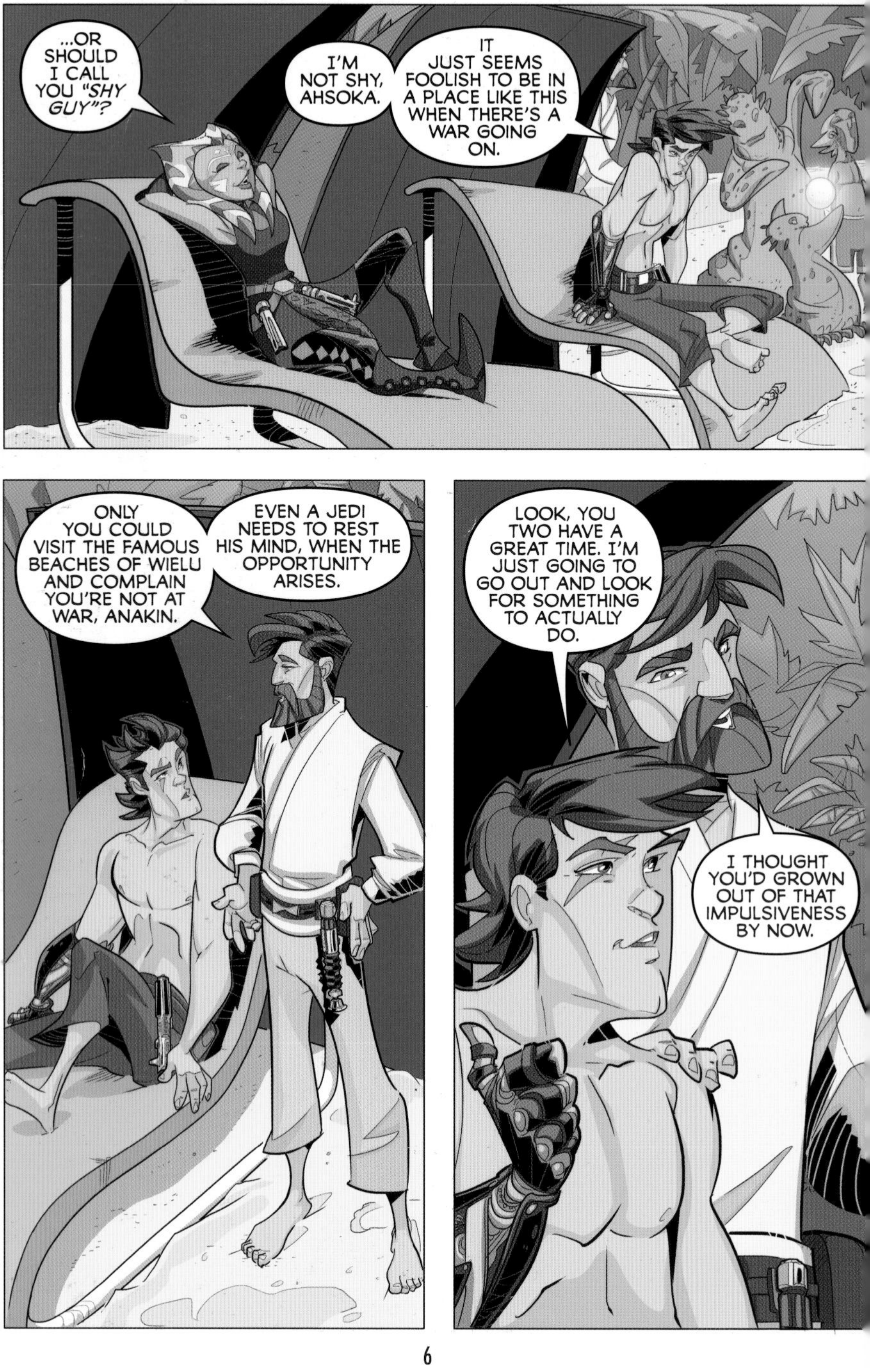
...OR SHOULD I CALL YOU *"SHY GUY"*?
I'M NOT SHY, AHSOKA.
IT JUST SEEMS FOOLISH TO BE IN A PLACE LIKE THIS WHEN THERE'S A WAR GOING ON.
ONLY YOU COULD VISIT THE FAMOUS BEACHES OF WIELU AND COMPLAIN YOU'RE NOT AT WAR, ANAKIN.
EVEN A JEDI NEEDS TO REST HIS MIND, WHEN THE OPPORTUNITY ARISES.
LOOK, YOU TWO HAVE A GREAT TIME. I'M JUST GOING TO GO OUT AND LOOK FOR SOMETHING TO ACTUALLY DO.
I THOUGHT YOU'D GROWN OUT OF THAT IMPULSIVENESS BY NOW.

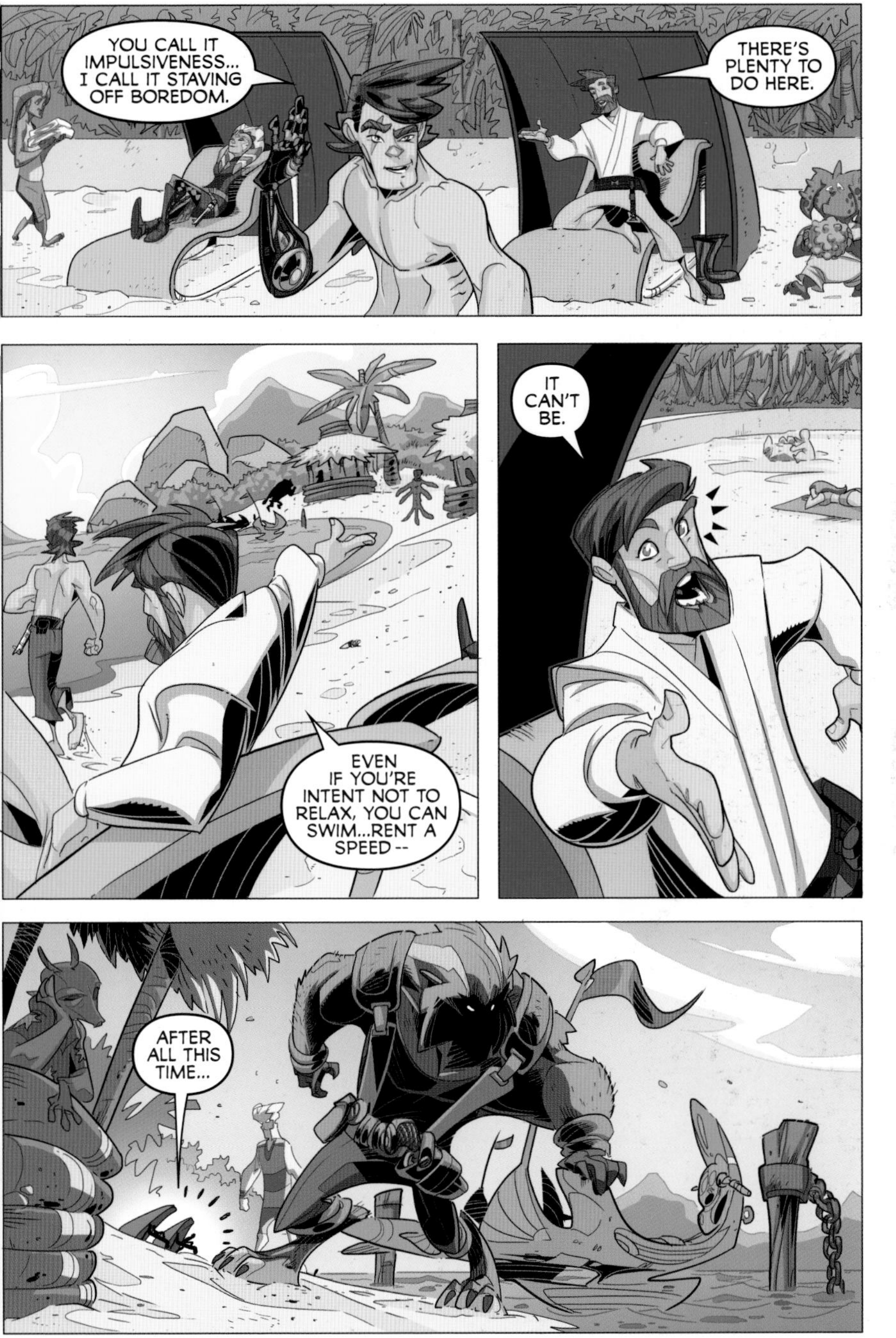
YOU CALL IT IMPULSIVENESS... I CALL IT STAVING OFF BOREDOM.
THERE'S PLENTY TO DO HERE.
EVEN IF YOU'RE INTENT NOT TO RELAX, YOU CAN SWIM...RENT A SPEED --
IT CAN'T BE.
AFTER ALL THIS TIME...

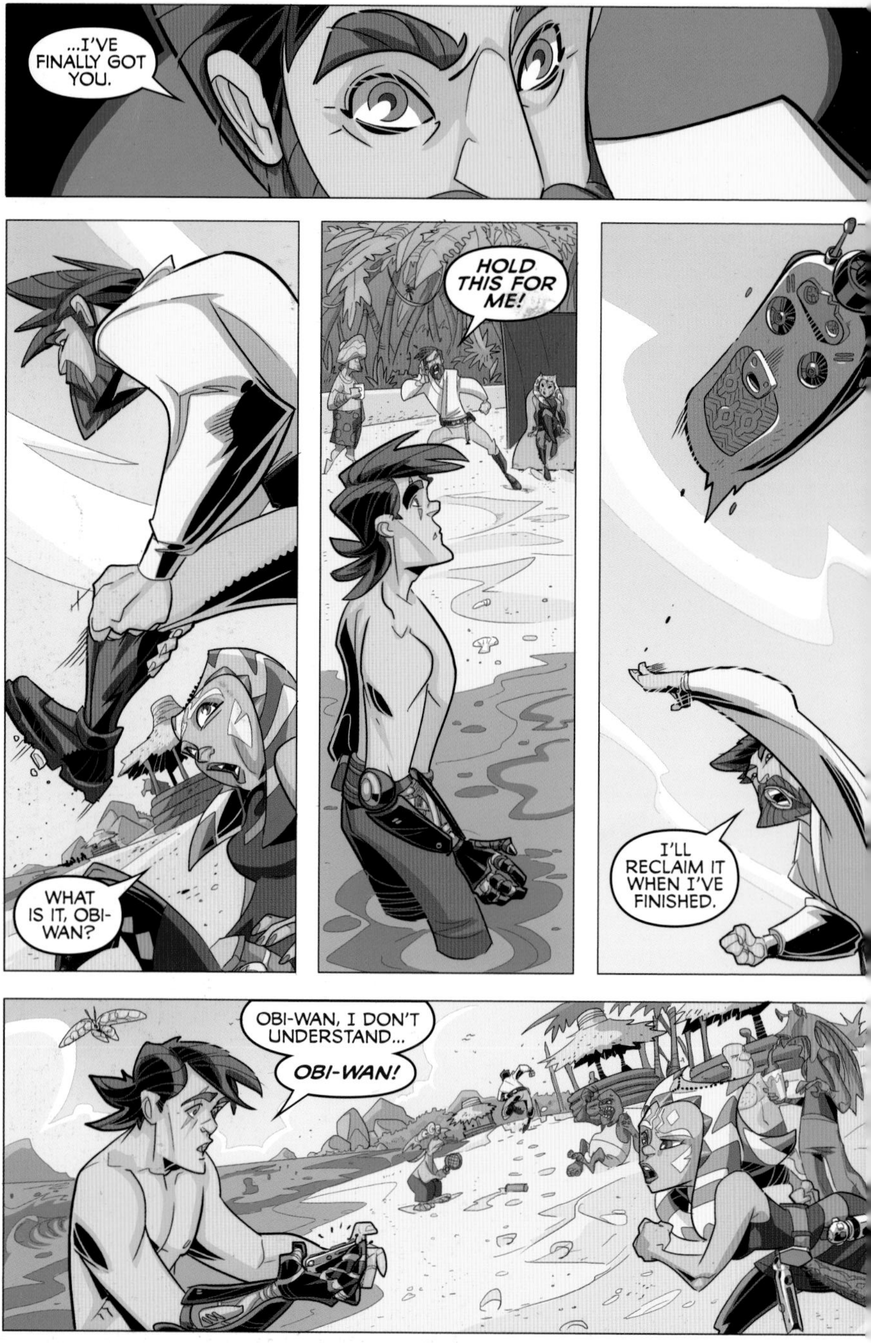
...I'VE FINALLY GOT YOU.
WHAT IS IT, OBI-WAN?
HOLD THIS FOR ME!
I'LL RECLAIM IT WHEN I'VE FINISHED.
OBI-WAN, I DON'T UNDERSTAND...
OBI-WAN!

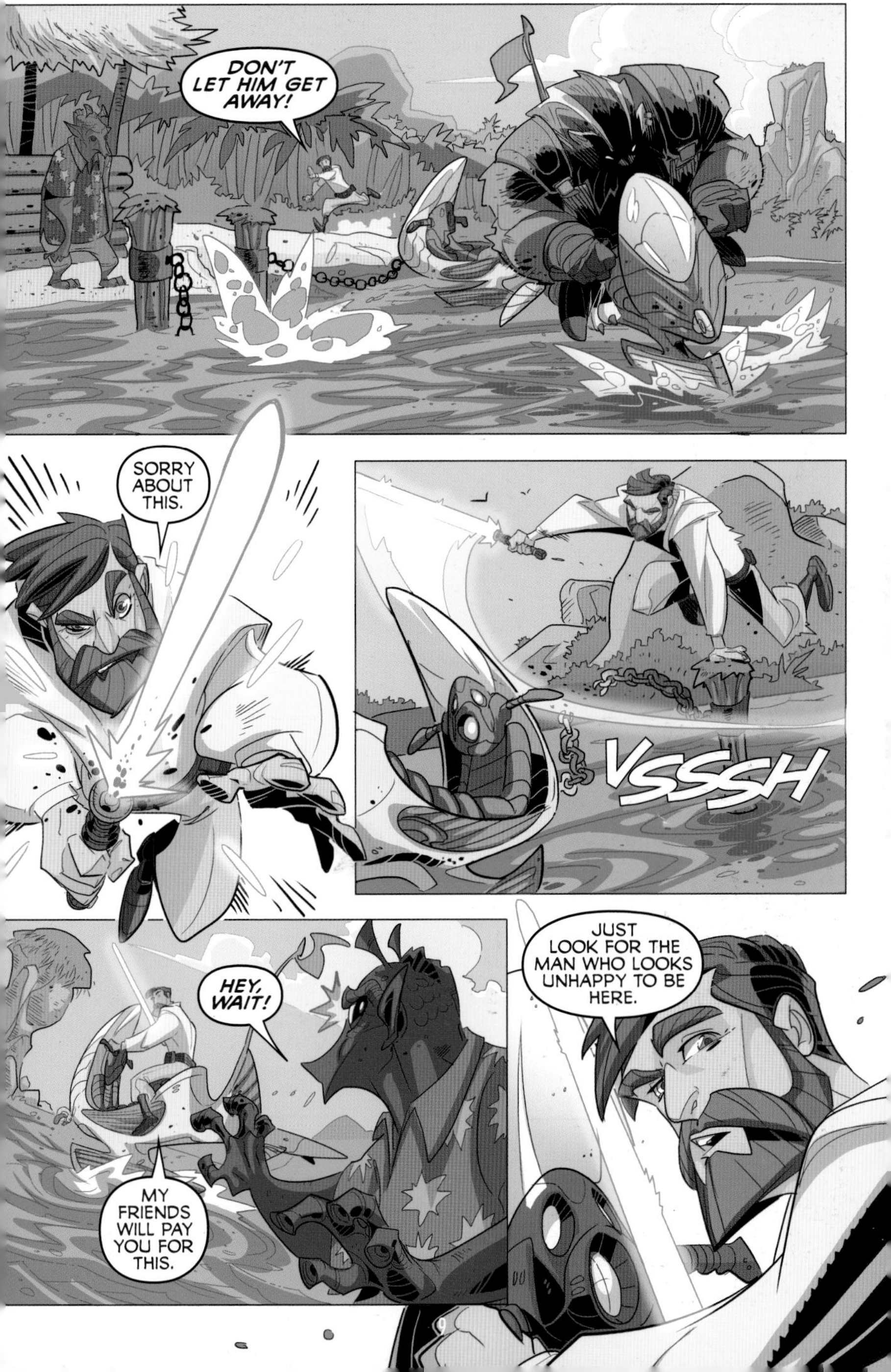
DON'T LET HIM GET AWAY!
SORRY ABOUT THIS.
VSSSH
HEY, WAIT!
MY FRIENDS WILL PAY YOU FOR THIS.
JUST LOOK FOR THE MAN WHO LOOKS UNHAPPY TO BE HERE.

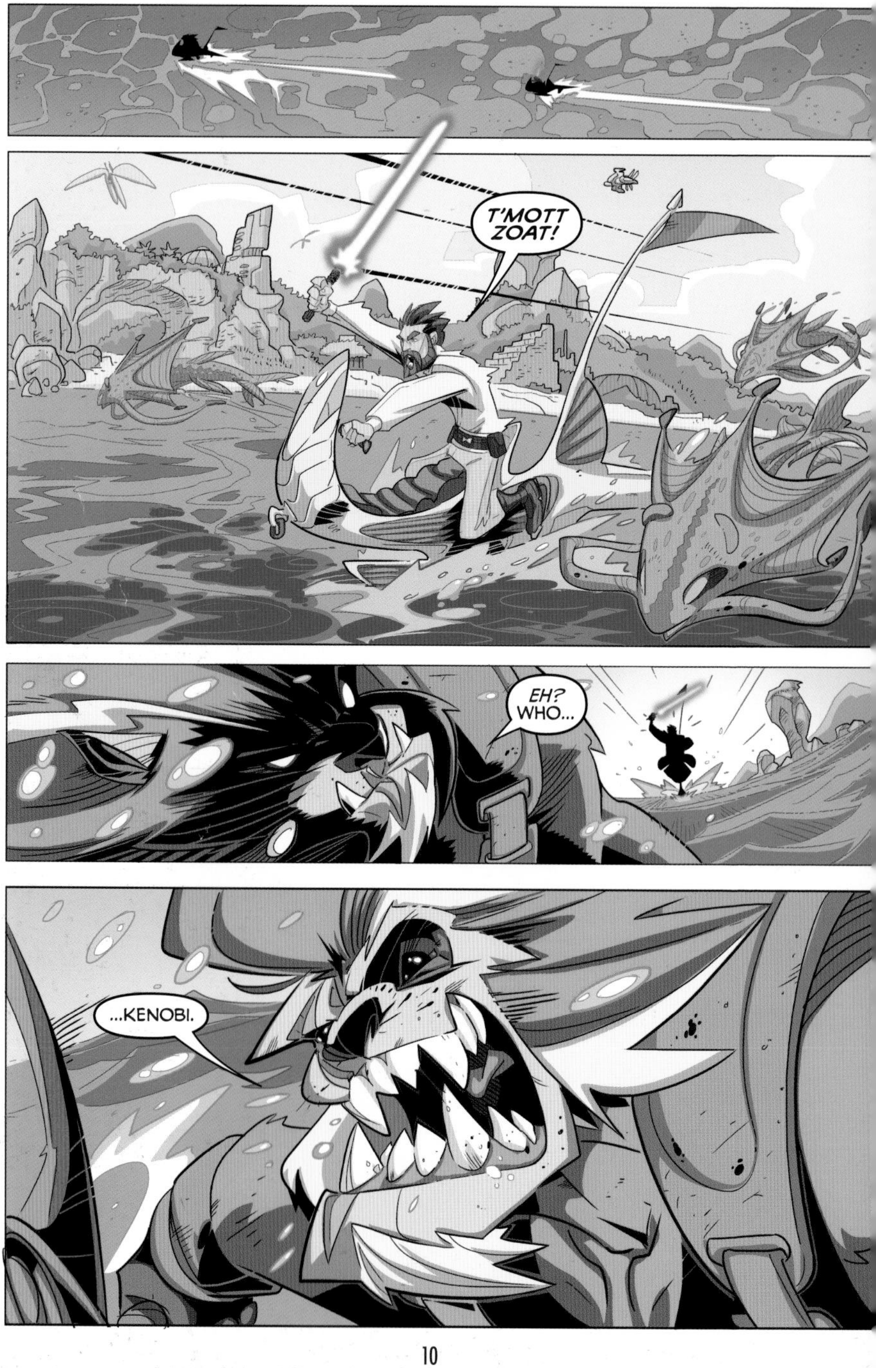
T'MOTT ZOAT!
EH? WHO...
...KENOBI.

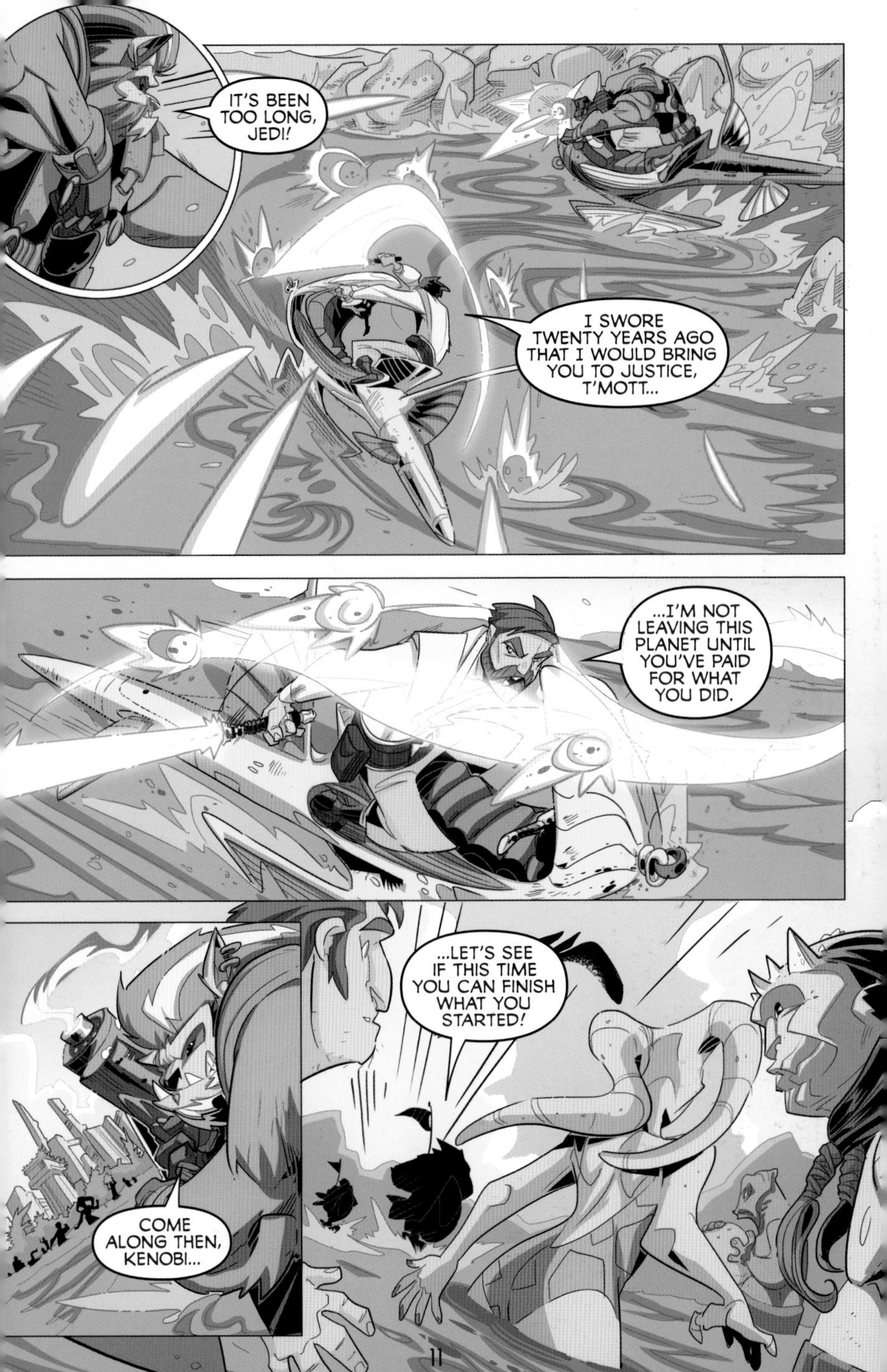
IT'S BEEN TOO LONG, JEDI!
I SWORE TWENTY YEARS AGO THAT I WOULD BRING YOU TO JUSTICE, T'MOTT...
...I'M NOT LEAVING THIS PLANET UNTIL YOU'VE PAID FOR WHAT YOU DID.
COME ALONG THEN, KENOBI...
...LET'S SEE IF THIS TIME YOU CAN FINISH WHAT YOU STARTED!

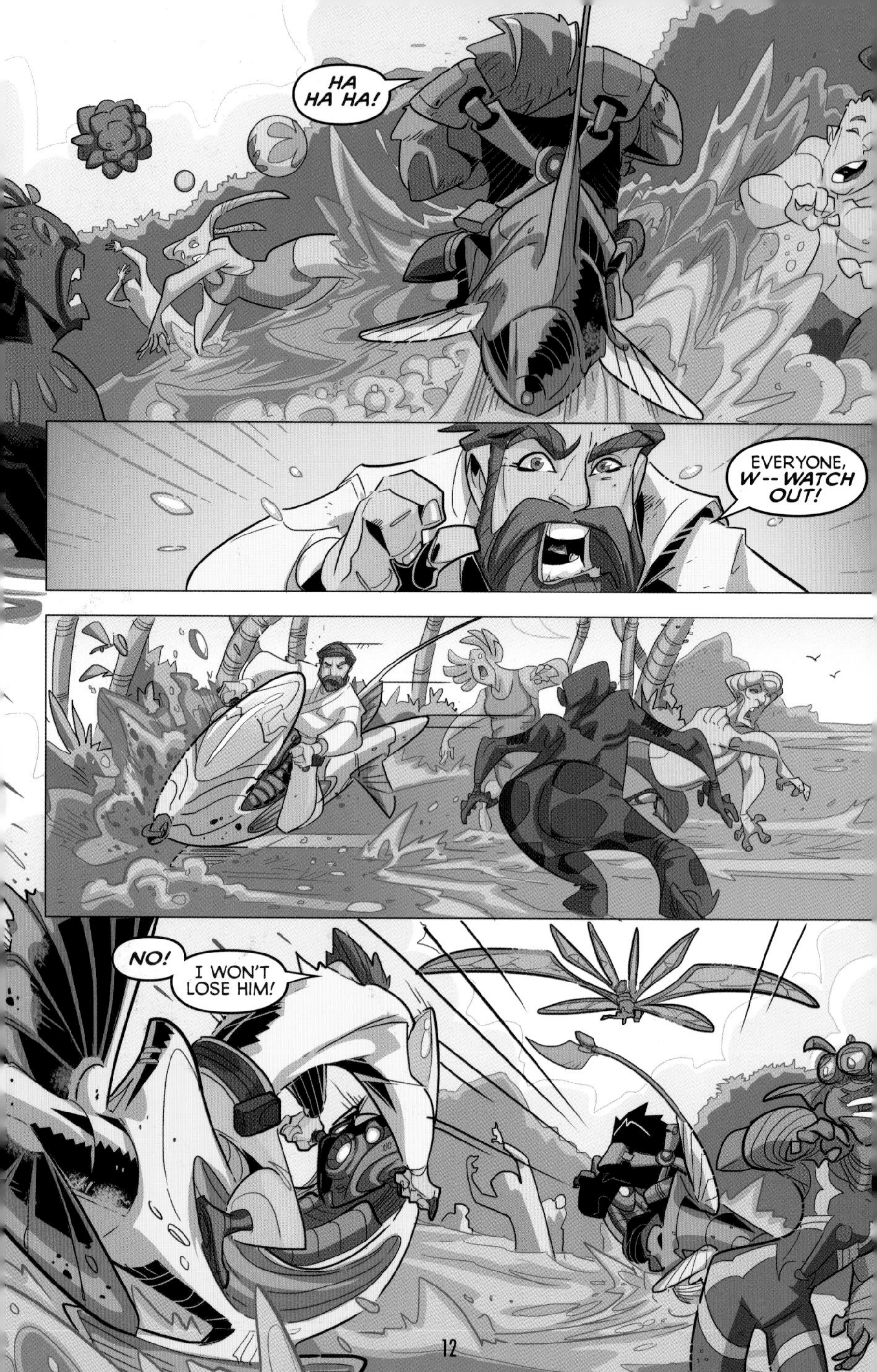
HA HA HA!
EVERYONE, W-- WATCH OUT!
NO!
I WON'T LOSE HIM!

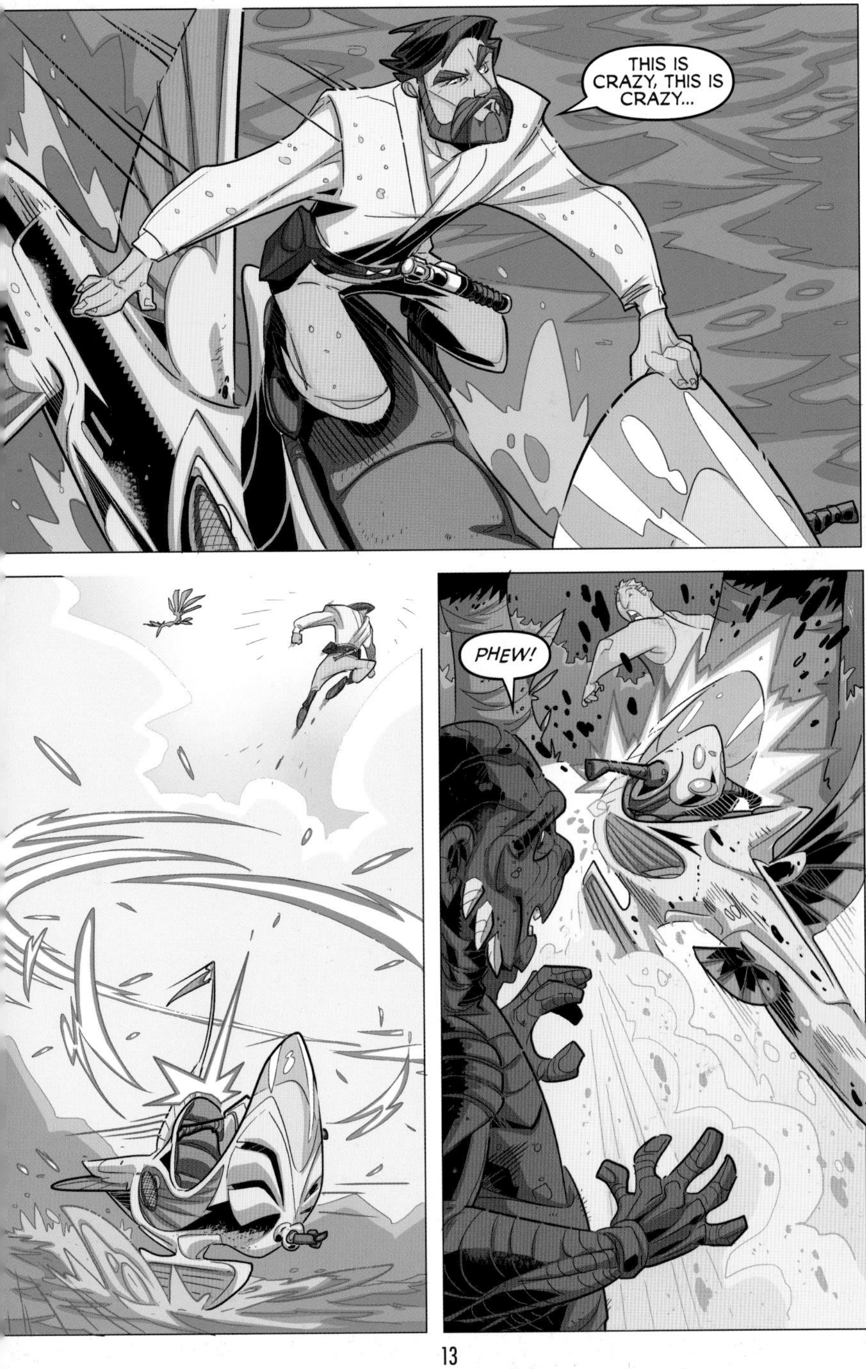
THIS IS CRAZY, THIS IS CRAZY...
PHEW!

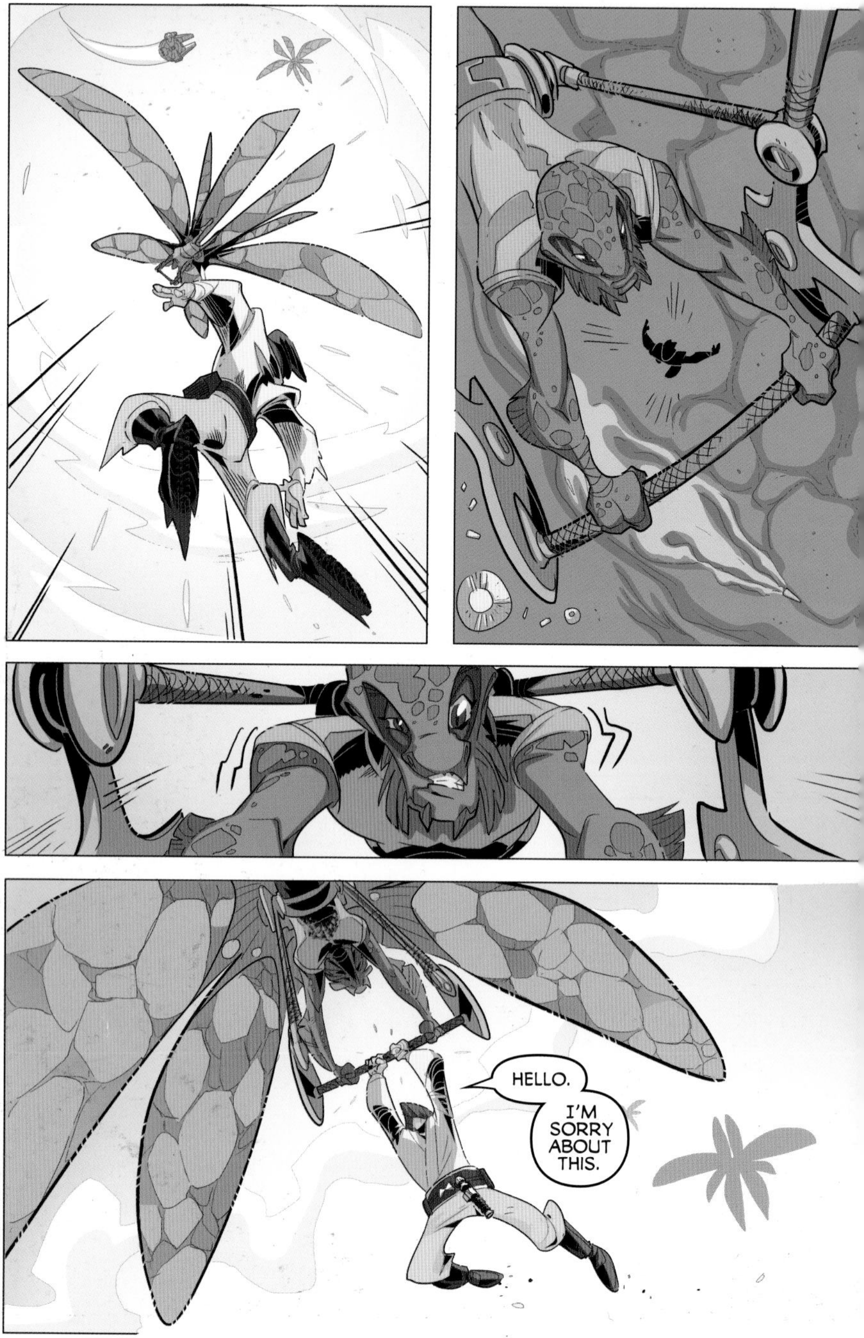
HELLO.
I'M SORRY ABOUT THIS.

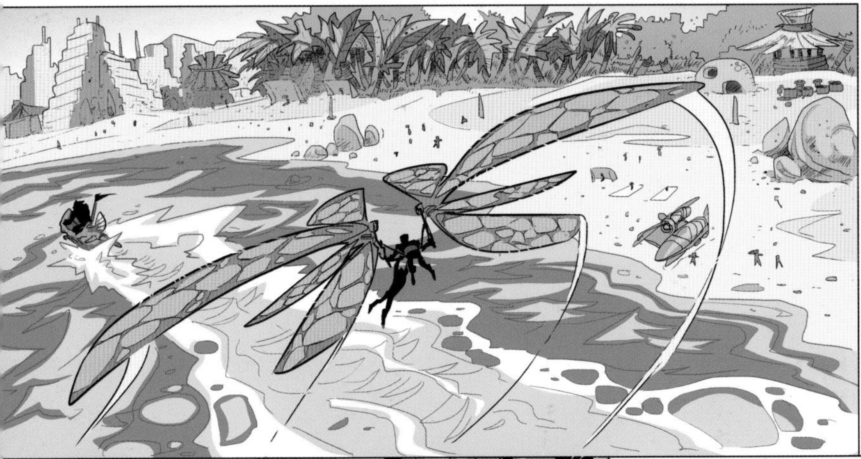

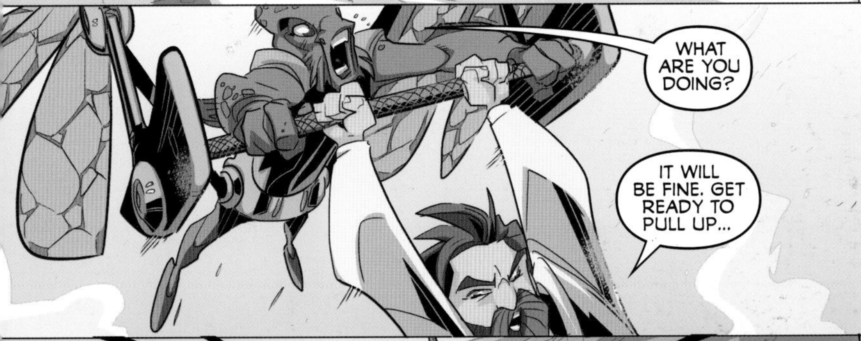
WHAT ARE YOU DOING?
IT WILL BE FINE. GET READY TO PULL UP...

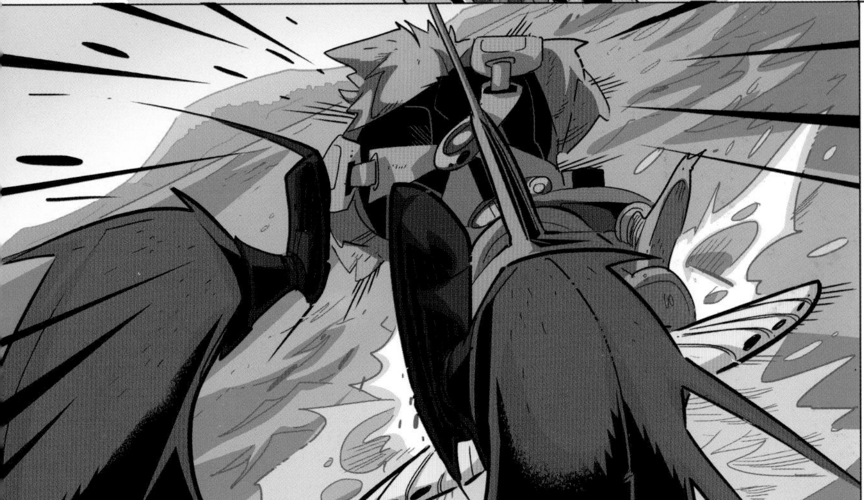

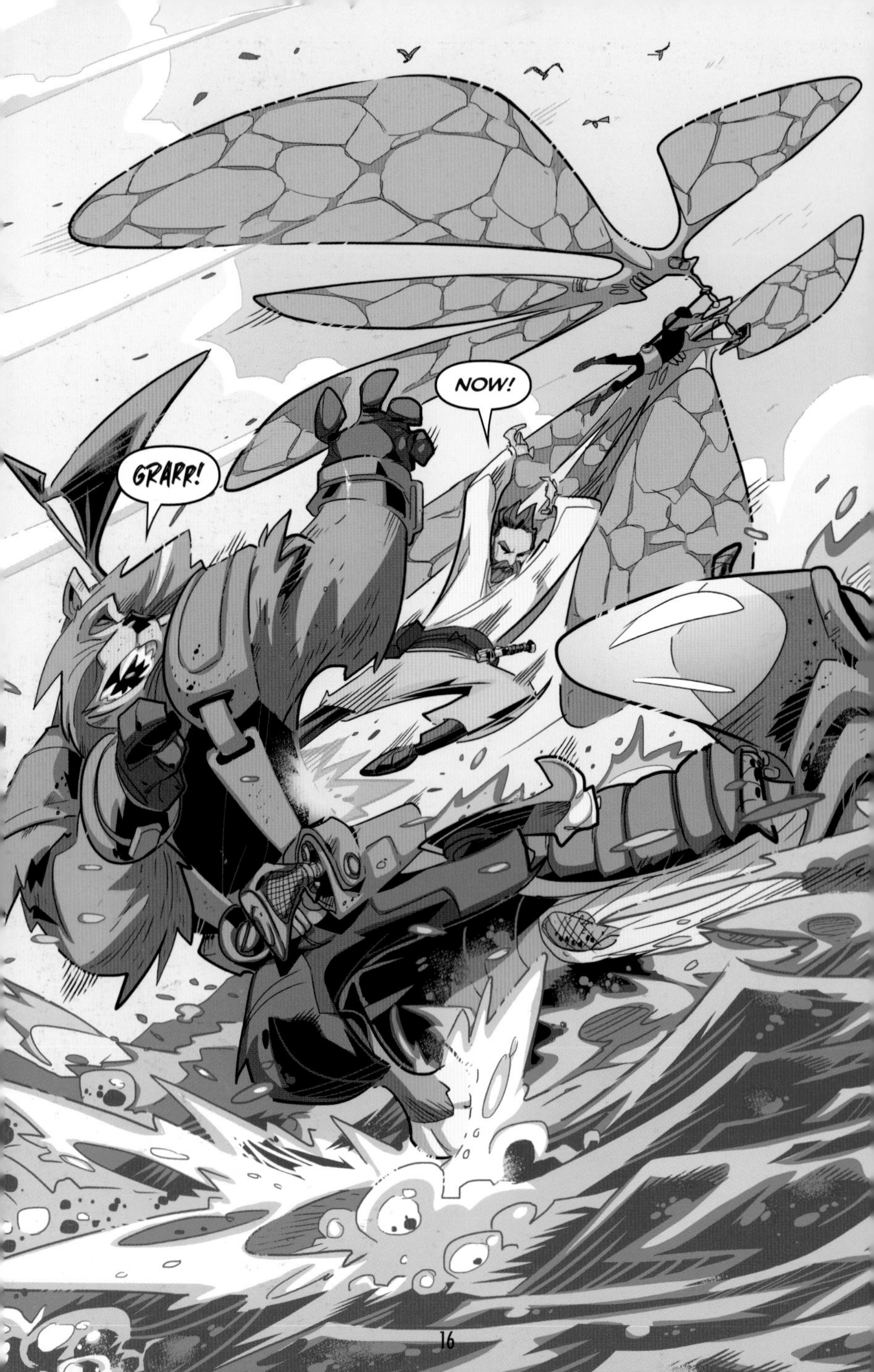
NOW!
GRARR!

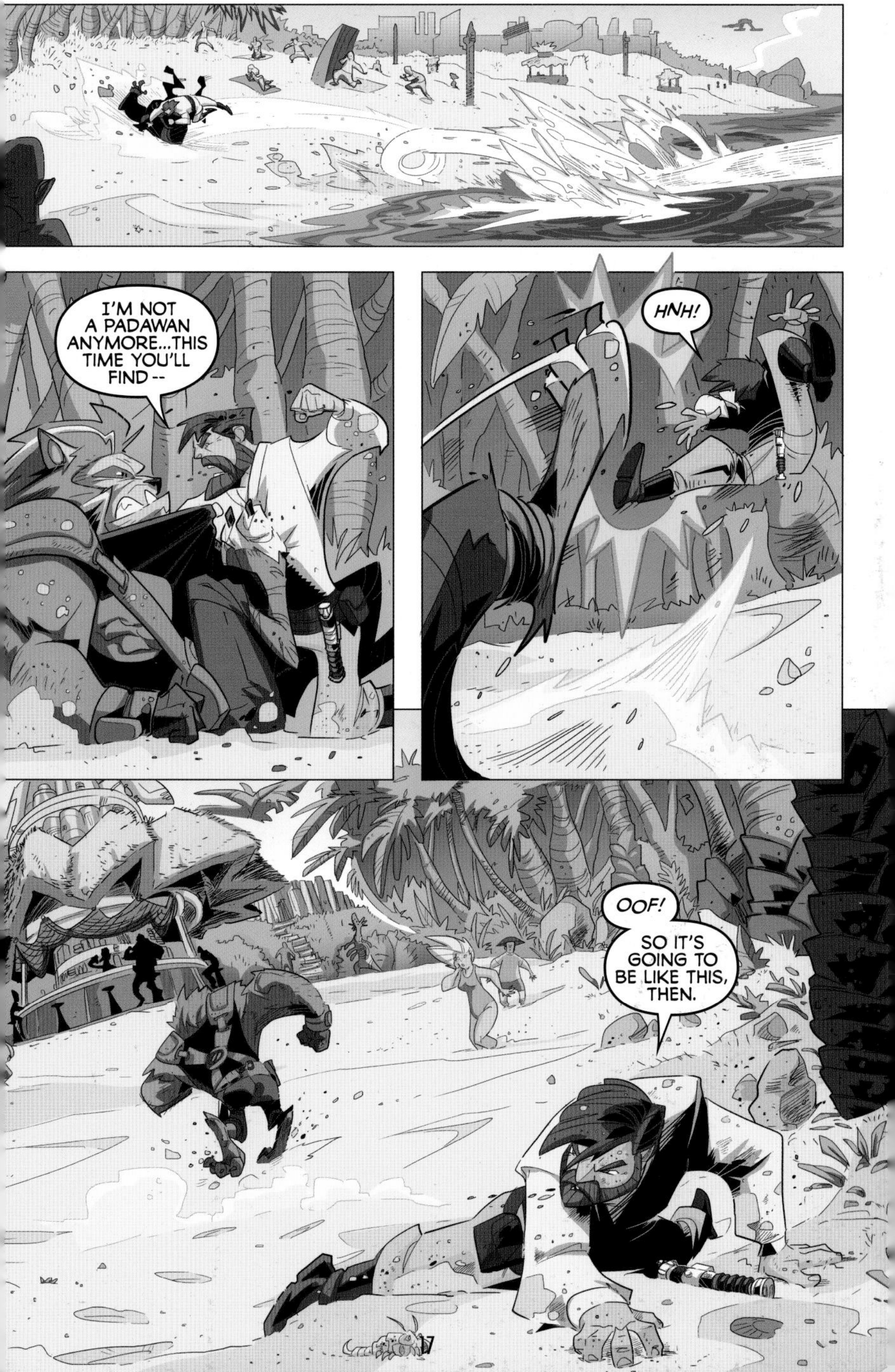
I'M NOT A PADAWAN ANYMORE...THIS TIME YOU'LL FIND --
HNH!
OOF!
SO IT'S GOING TO BE LIKE THIS, THEN.

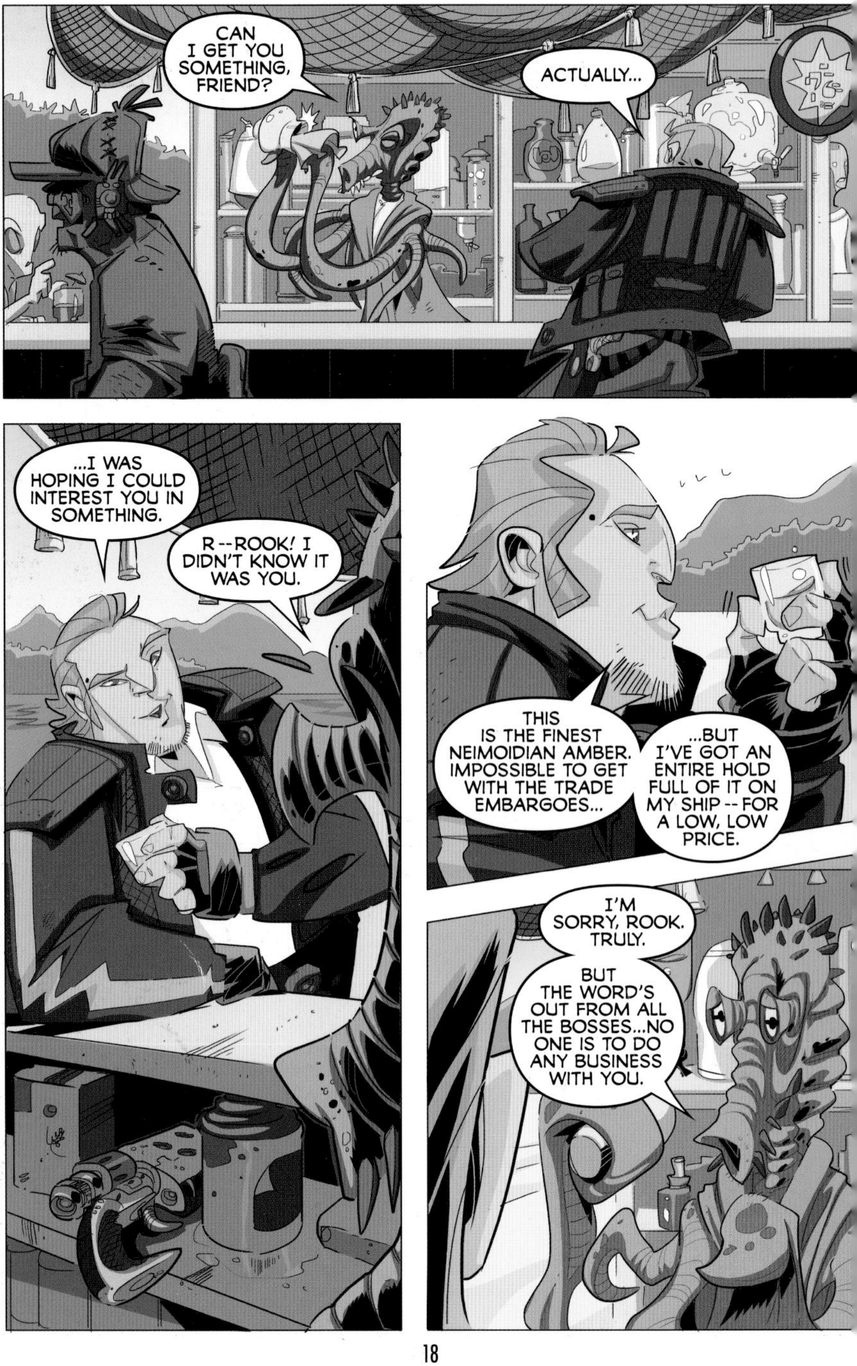
CAN I GET YOU SOMETHING, FRIEND?
ACTUALLY...
...I WAS HOPING I COULD INTEREST YOU IN SOMETHING.
R--ROOK! I DIDN'T KNOW IT WAS YOU.
THIS IS THE FINEST NEIMOIDIAN AMBER. IMPOSSIBLE TO GET WITH THE TRADE EMBARGOES...
...BUT I'VE GOT AN ENTIRE HOLD FULL OF IT ON MY SHIP--FOR A LOW, LOW PRICE.
I'M SORRY, ROOK. TRULY.
BUT THE WORD'S OUT FROM ALL THE BOSSES...NO ONE IS TO DO ANY BUSINESS WITH YOU.

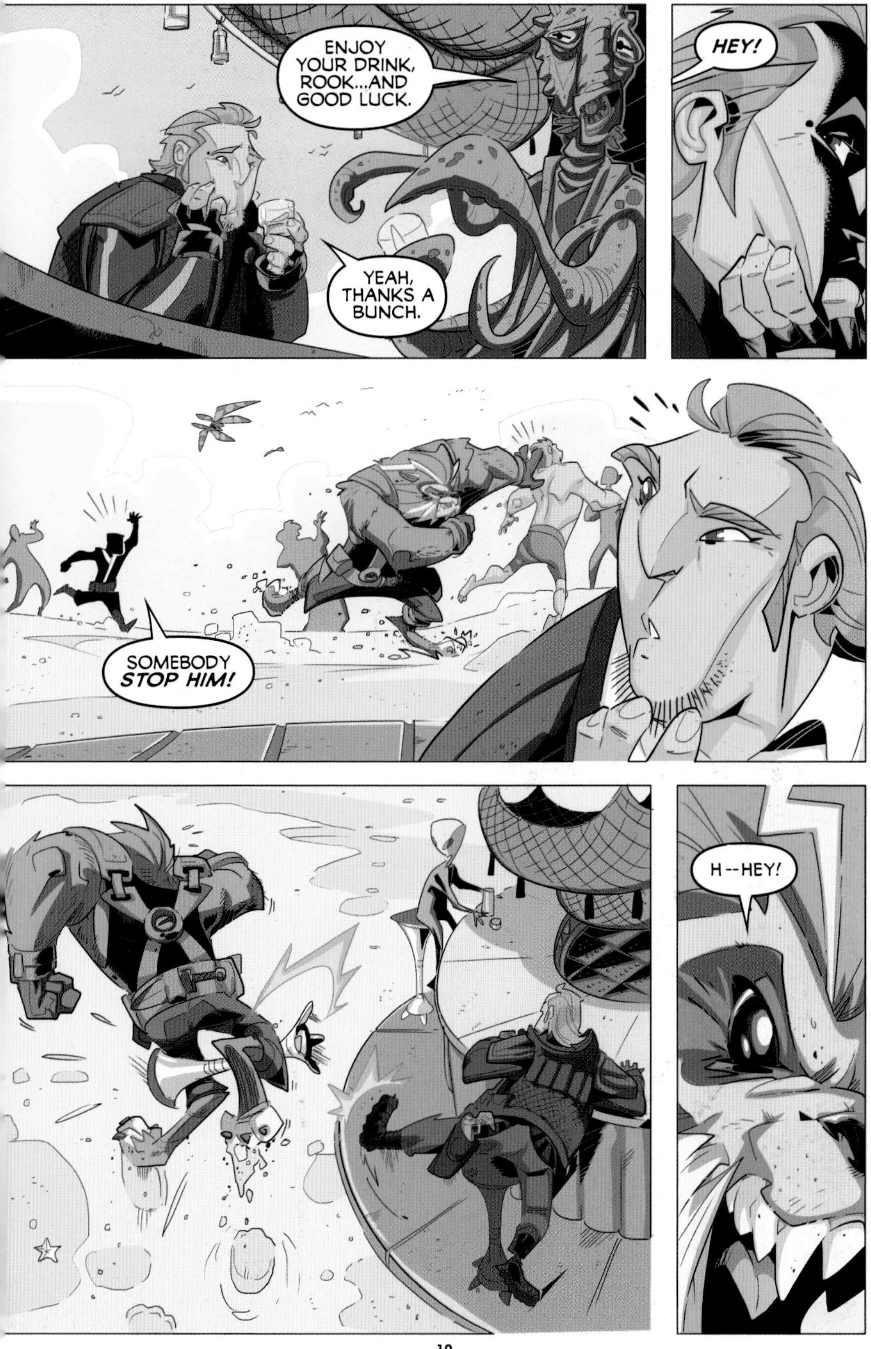
ENJOY YOUR DRINK, ROOK...AND GOOD LUCK.
YEAH, THANKS A BUNCH.
HEY!
SOMEBODY STOP HIM!
H--HEY!

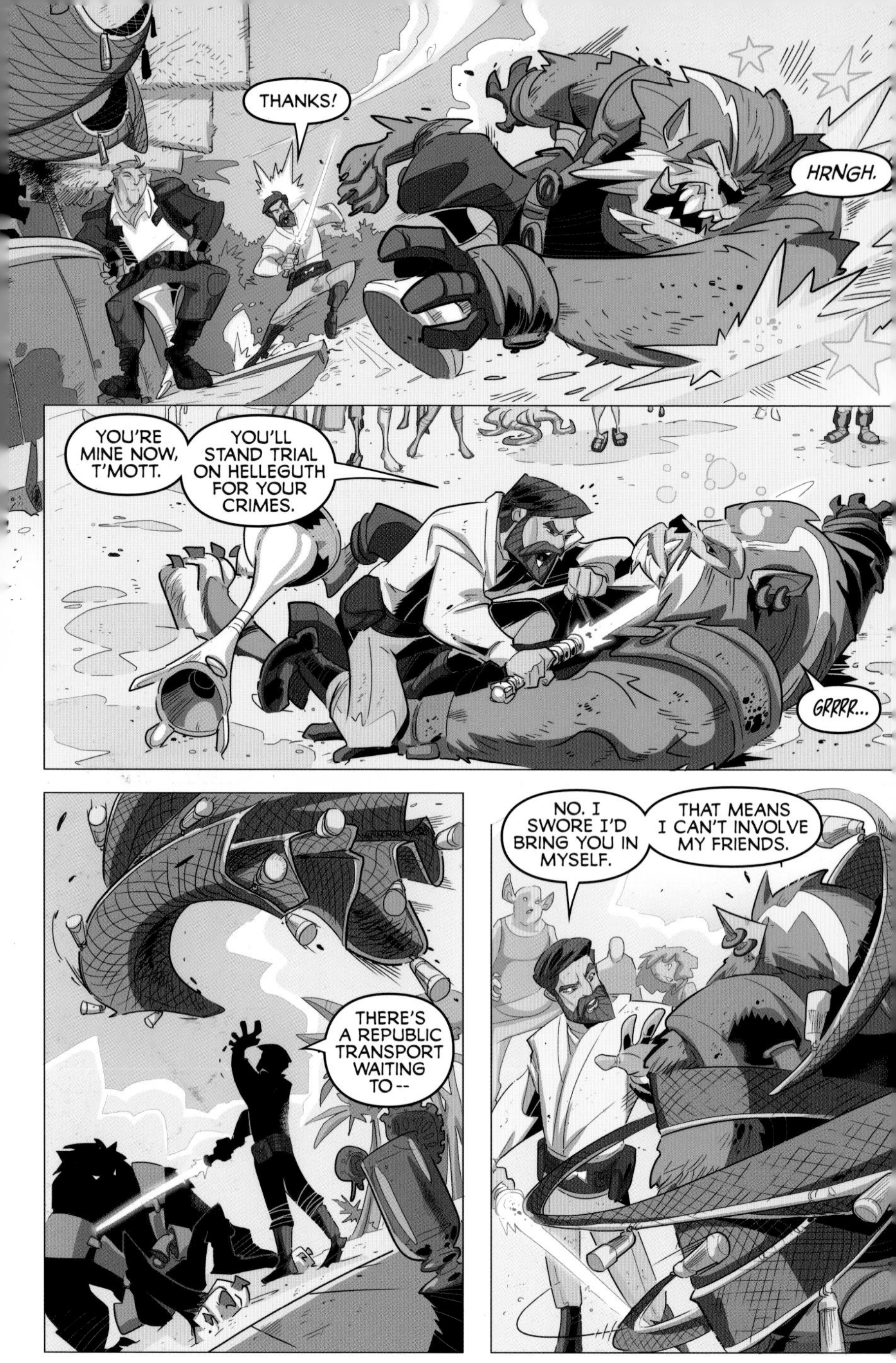
THANKS!
HRNGH.
YOU'RE MINE NOW, T'MOTT.
YOU'LL STAND TRIAL ON HELLEGUTH FOR YOUR CRIMES.
GRRRR...
THERE'S A REPUBLIC TRANSPORT WAITING TO --
NO. I SWORE I'D BRING YOU IN MYSELF.
THAT MEANS I CAN'T INVOLVE MY FRIENDS.

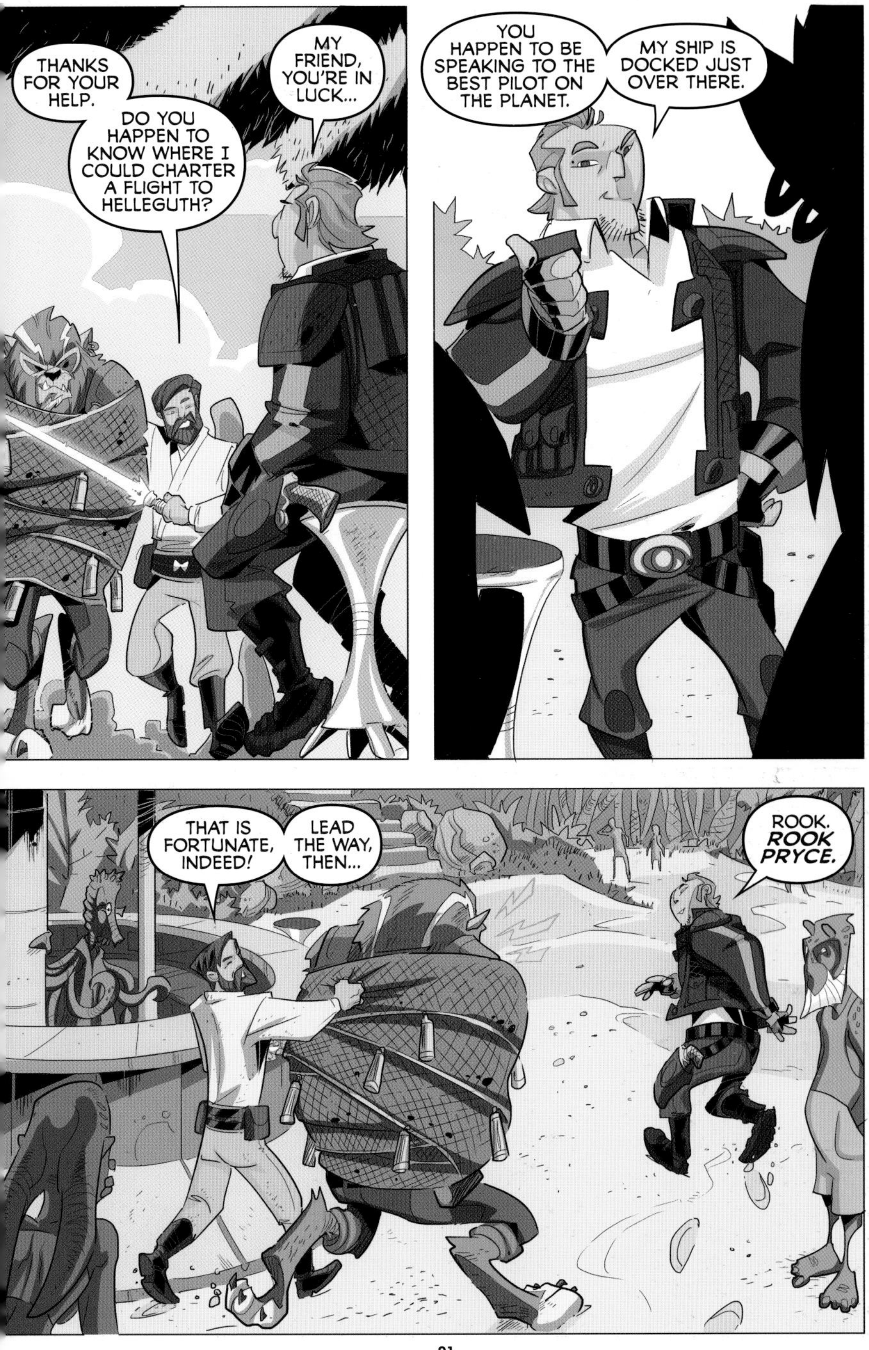
THANKS FOR YOUR HELP.
DO YOU HAPPEN TO KNOW WHERE I COULD CHARTER A FLIGHT TO HELLEGUTH?
MY FRIEND, YOU'RE IN LUCK...
YOU HAPPEN TO BE SPEAKING TO THE BEST PILOT ON THE PLANET.
MY SHIP IS DOCKED JUST OVER THERE.
THAT IS FORTUNATE, INDEED!
LEAD THE WAY, THEN...
ROOK. *ROOK PRYCE.*

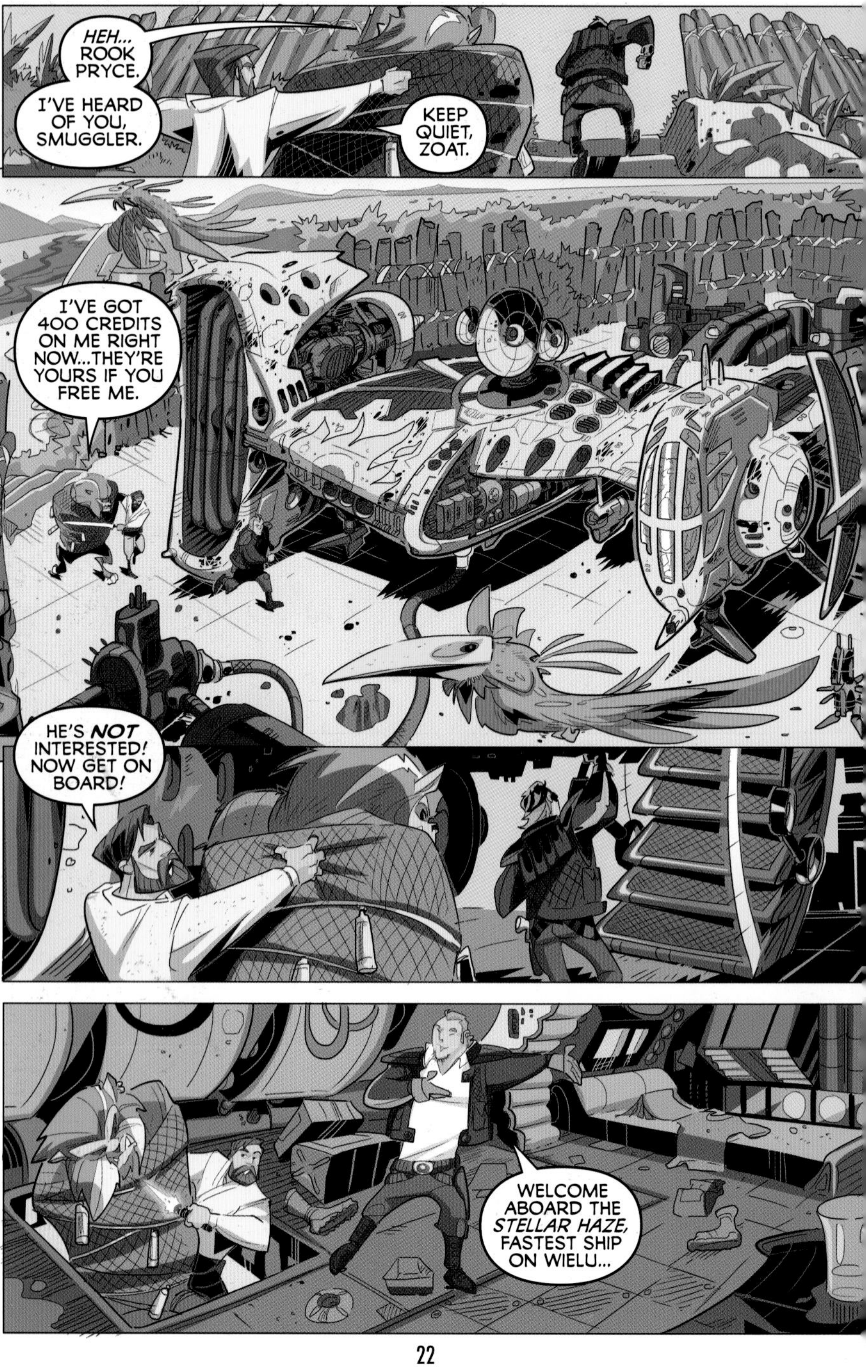
HEH... ROOK PRYCE.
I'VE HEARD OF YOU, SMUGGLER.
KEEP QUIET, ZOAT.
I'VE GOT 400 CREDITS ON ME RIGHT NOW...THEY'RE YOURS IF YOU FREE ME.
HE'S **NOT** INTERESTED! NOW GET ON BOARD!
WELCOME ABOARD THE *STELLAR HAZE,* FASTEST SHIP ON WIELU...

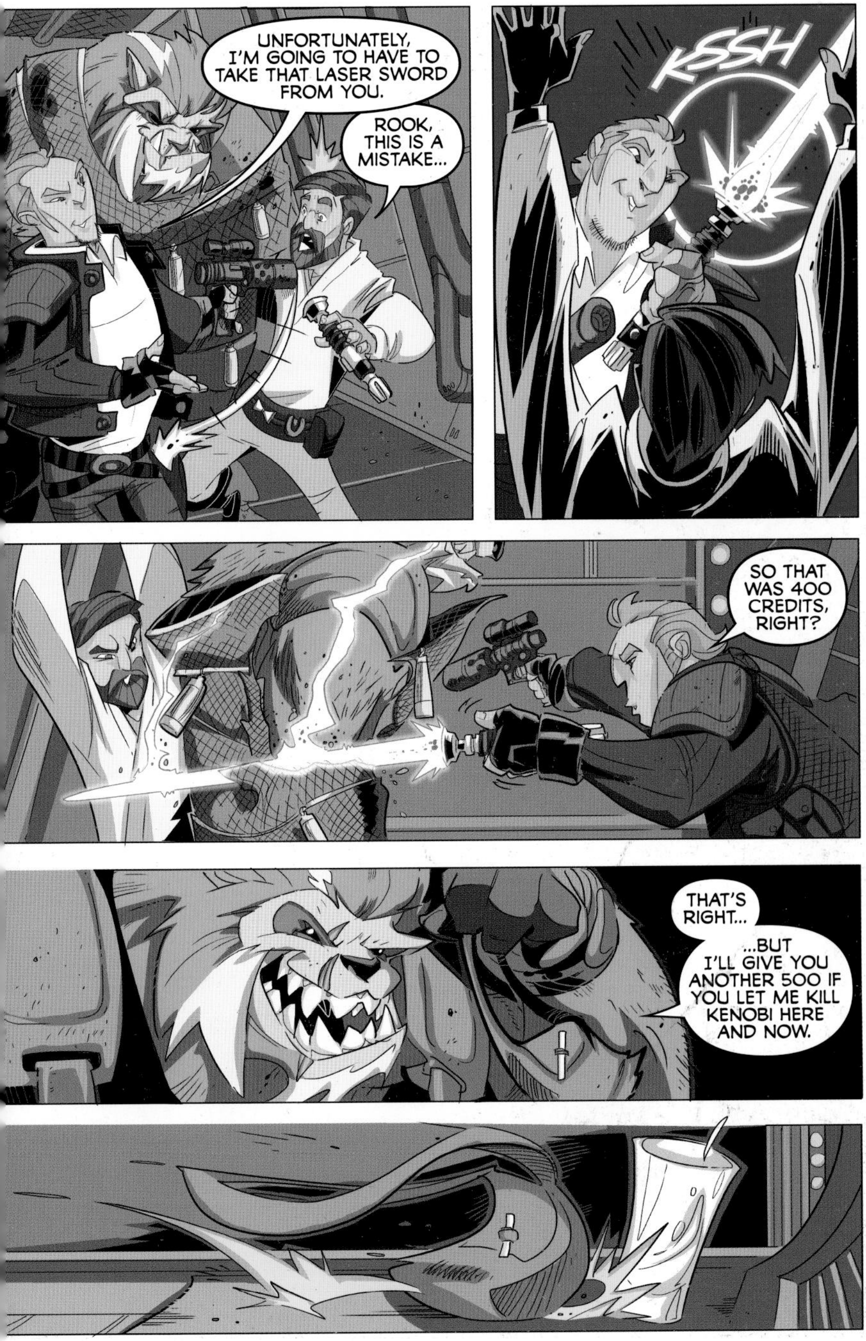
UNFORTUNATELY, I'M GOING TO HAVE TO TAKE THAT LASER SWORD FROM YOU.
ROOK, THIS IS A MISTAKE...
KSSH
SO THAT WAS 400 CREDITS, RIGHT?
THAT'S RIGHT...
...BUT I'LL GIVE YOU ANOTHER 500 IF YOU LET ME KILL KENOBI HERE AND NOW.

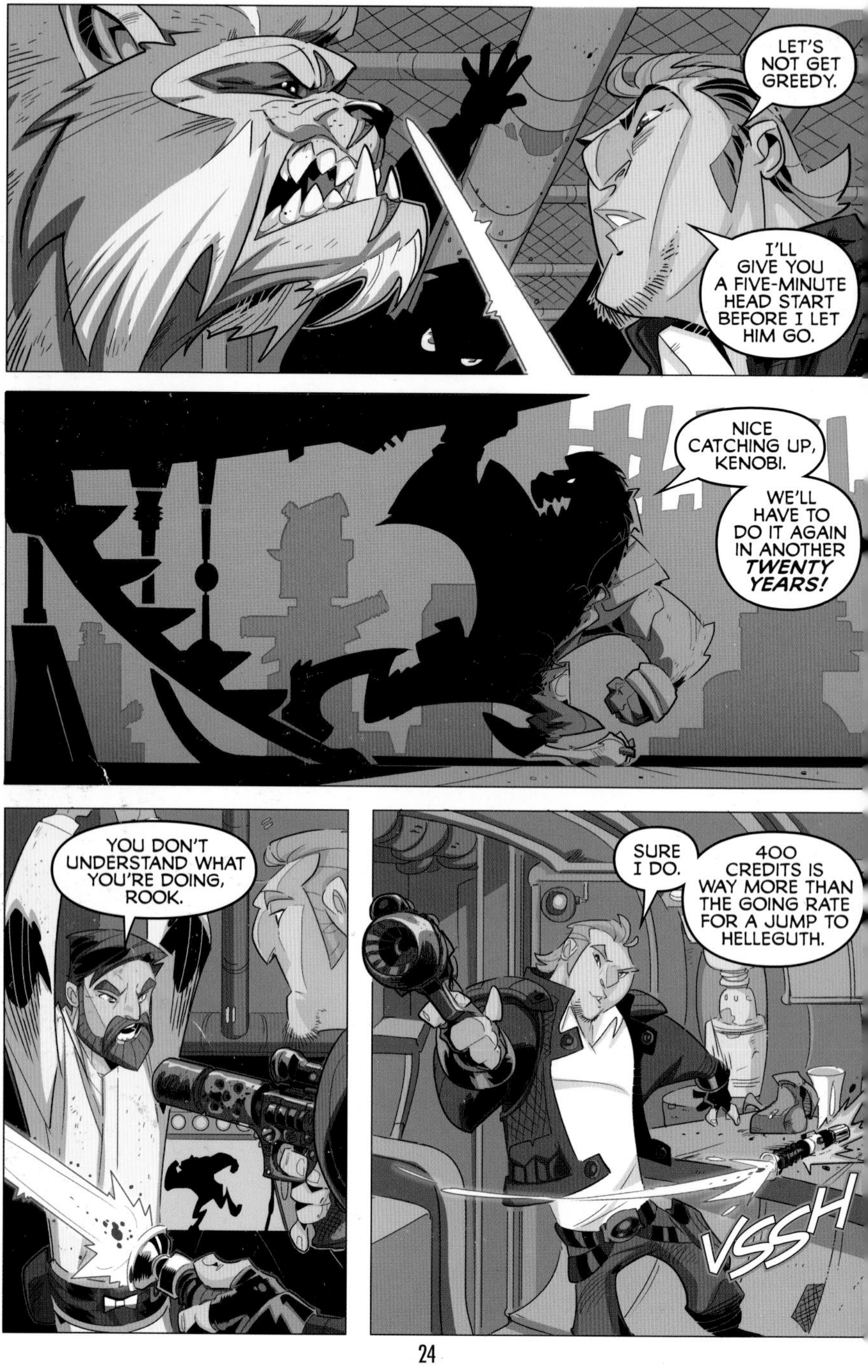
LET'S NOT GET GREEDY.
I'LL GIVE YOU A FIVE-MINUTE HEAD START BEFORE I LET HIM GO.
NICE CATCHING UP, KENOBI.
WE'LL HAVE TO DO IT AGAIN IN ANOTHER ***TWENTY YEARS!***
YOU DON'T UNDERSTAND WHAT YOU'RE DOING, ROOK.
SURE I DO.
400 CREDITS IS WAY MORE THAN THE GOING RATE FOR A JUMP TO HELLEGUTH.
VSSH

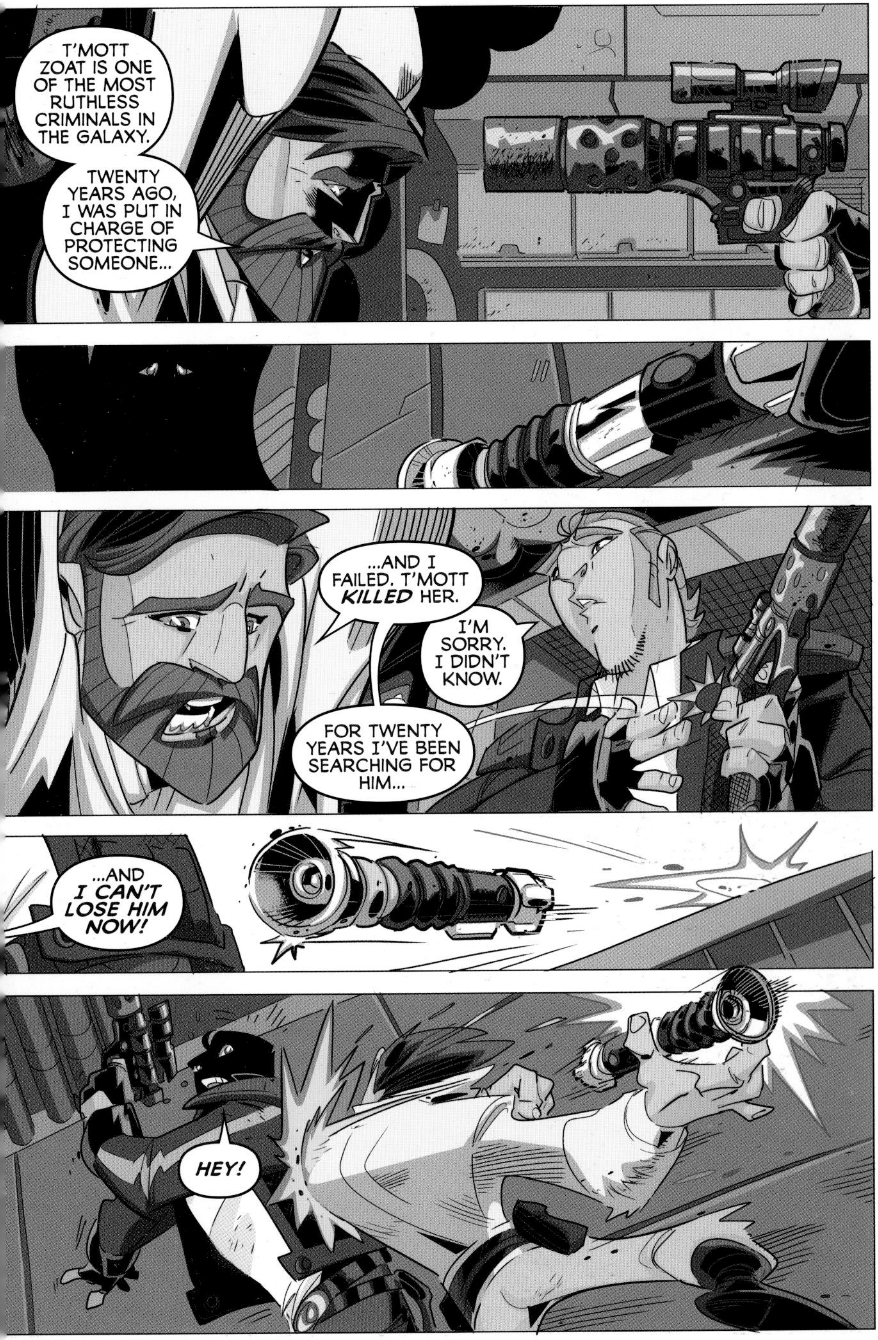
T'MOTT ZOAT IS ONE OF THE MOST RUTHLESS CRIMINALS IN THE GALAXY.
TWENTY YEARS AGO, I WAS PUT IN CHARGE OF PROTECTING SOMEONE...
...AND I FAILED. T'MOTT *KILLED* HER.
I'M SORRY. I DIDN'T KNOW.
FOR TWENTY YEARS I'VE BEEN SEARCHING FOR HIM...
...AND *I CAN'T LOSE HIM NOW!*
HEY!

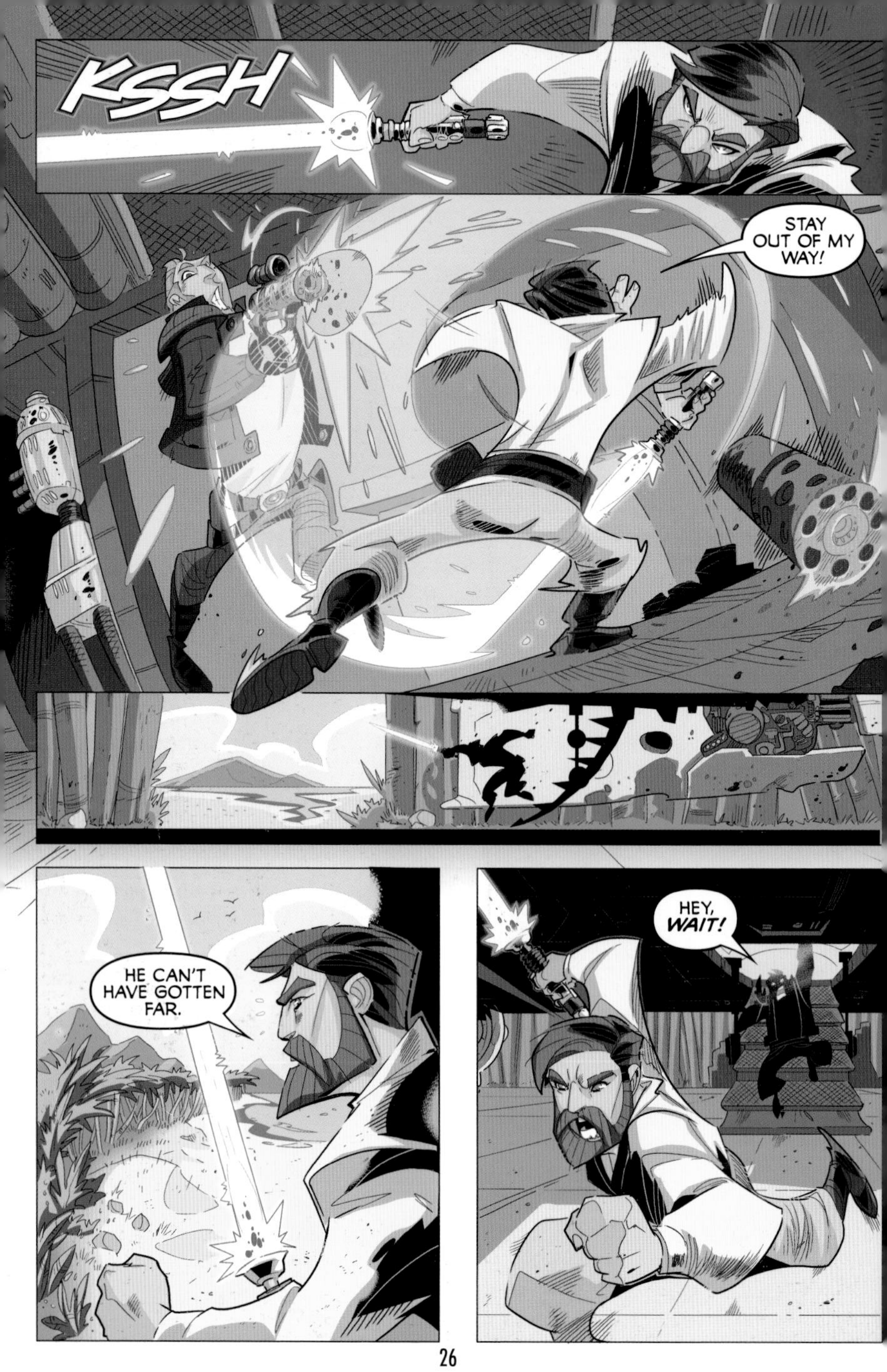
KSSH
STAY OUT OF MY WAY!
HE CAN'T HAVE GOTTEN FAR.
HEY, WAIT!

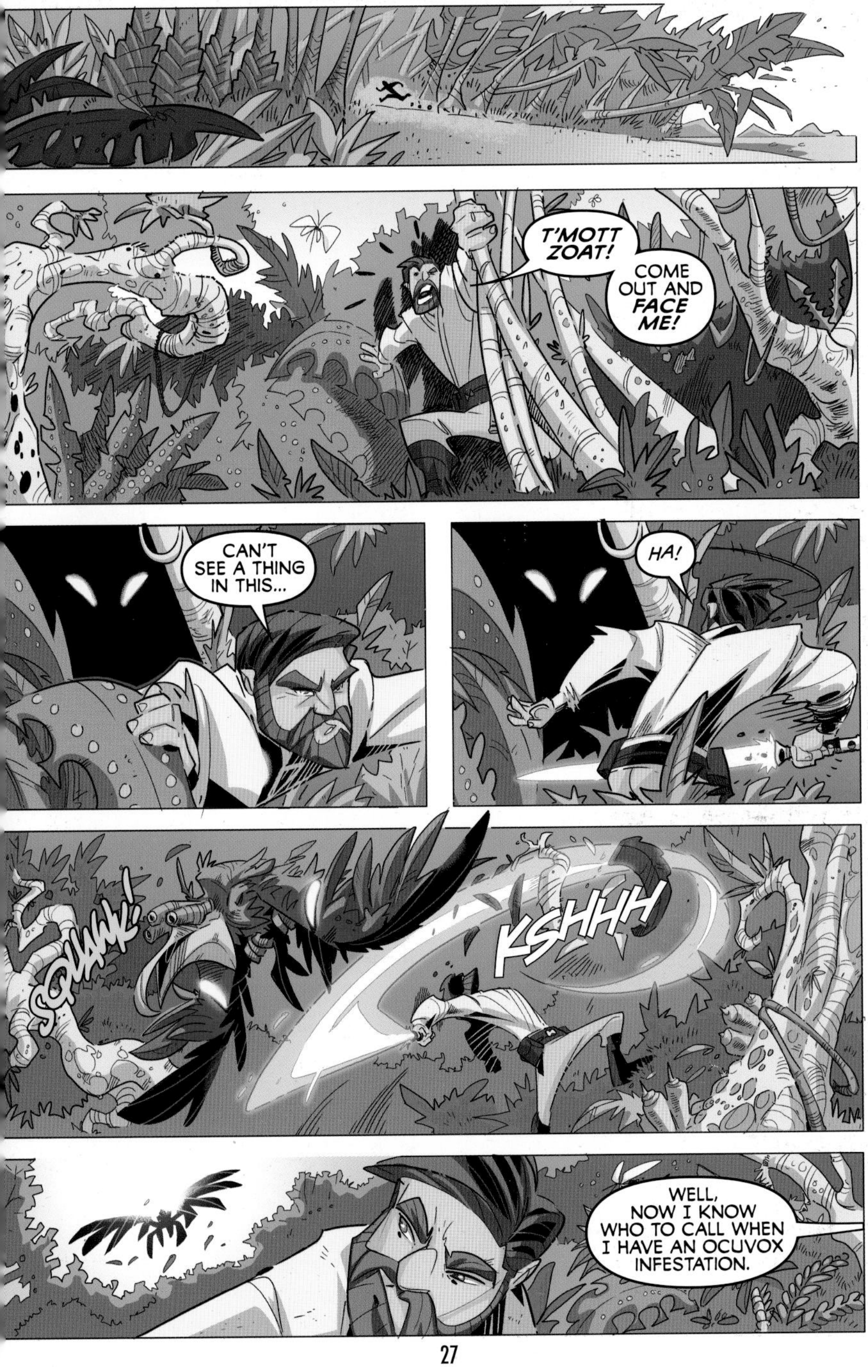
T'MOTT ZOAT!
COME OUT AND FACE ME!
CAN'T SEE A THING IN THIS...
HA!
SQUAWK!
KSHHH
WELL, NOW I KNOW WHO TO CALL WHEN I HAVE AN OCUVOX INFESTATION.

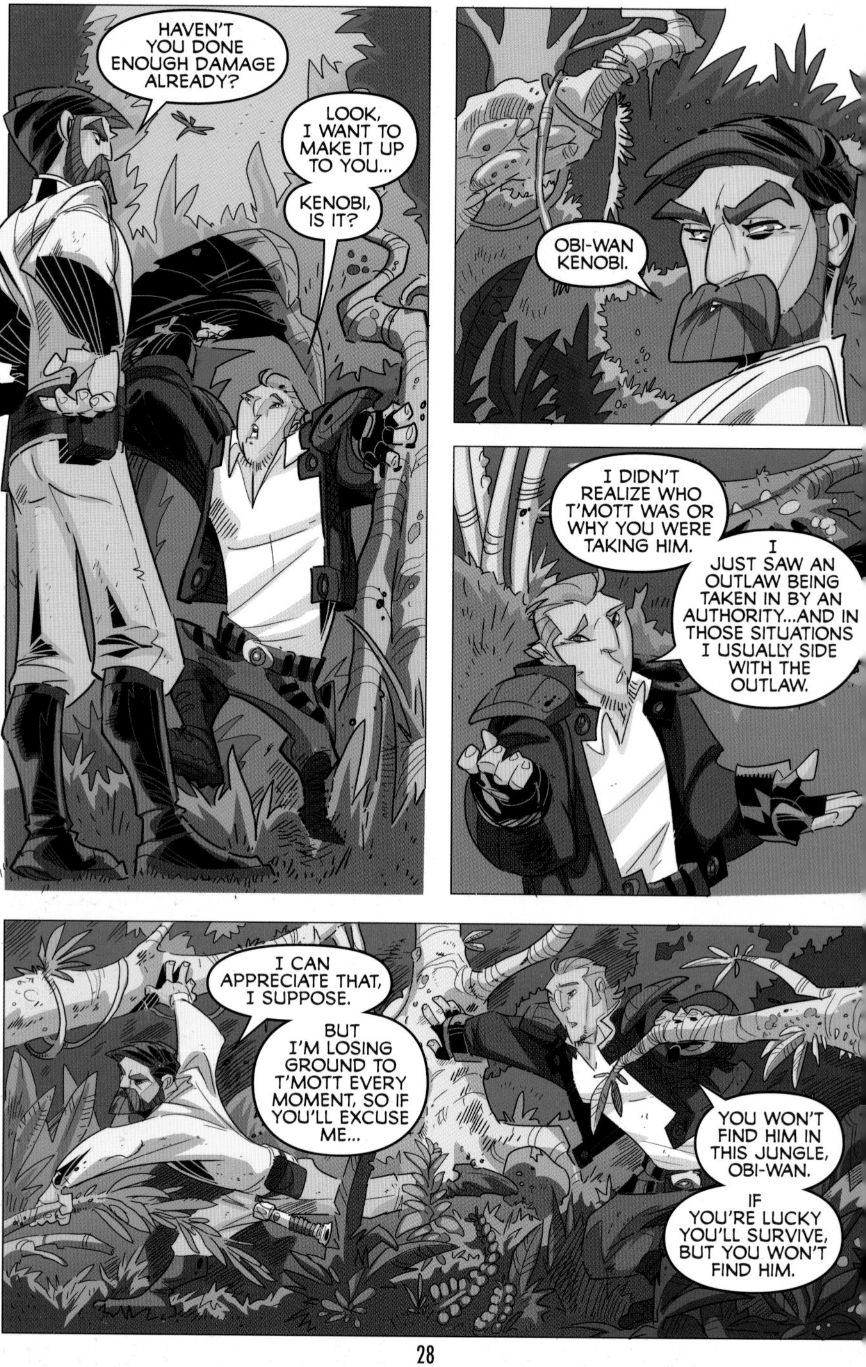
HAVEN'T YOU DONE ENOUGH DAMAGE ALREADY?
LOOK, I WANT TO MAKE IT UP TO YOU...
KENOBI, IS IT?
OBI-WAN KENOBI.
I DIDN'T REALIZE WHO T'MOTT WAS OR WHY YOU WERE TAKING HIM.
I JUST SAW AN OUTLAW BEING TAKEN IN BY AN AUTHORITY...AND IN THOSE SITUATIONS I USUALLY SIDE WITH THE OUTLAW.
I CAN APPRECIATE THAT, I SUPPOSE.
BUT I'M LOSING GROUND TO T'MOTT EVERY MOMENT, SO IF YOU'LL EXCUSE ME...
YOU WON'T FIND HIM IN THIS JUNGLE, OBI-WAN.
IF YOU'RE LUCKY YOU'LL SURVIVE, BUT YOU WON'T FIND HIM.

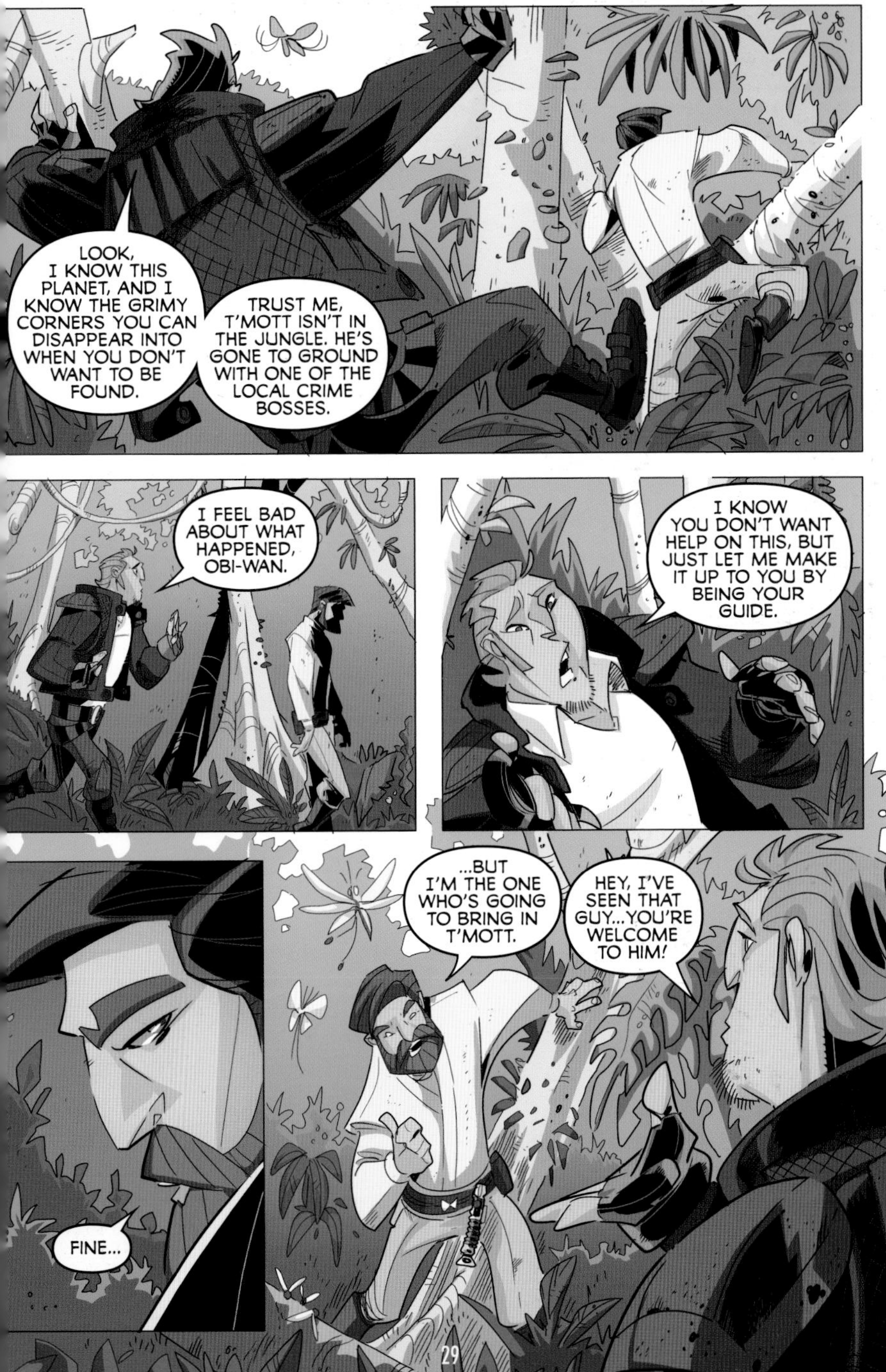
LOOK, I KNOW THIS PLANET, AND I KNOW THE GRIMY CORNERS YOU CAN DISAPPEAR INTO WHEN YOU DON'T WANT TO BE FOUND.
TRUST ME, T'MOTT ISN'T IN THE JUNGLE. HE'S GONE TO GROUND WITH ONE OF THE LOCAL CRIME BOSSES.
I FEEL BAD ABOUT WHAT HAPPENED, OBI-WAN.
I KNOW YOU DON'T WANT HELP ON THIS, BUT JUST LET ME MAKE IT UP TO YOU BY BEING YOUR GUIDE.
FINE...
...BUT I'M THE ONE WHO'S GOING TO BRING IN T'MOTT.
HEY, I'VE SEEN THAT GUY...YOU'RE WELCOME TO HIM!

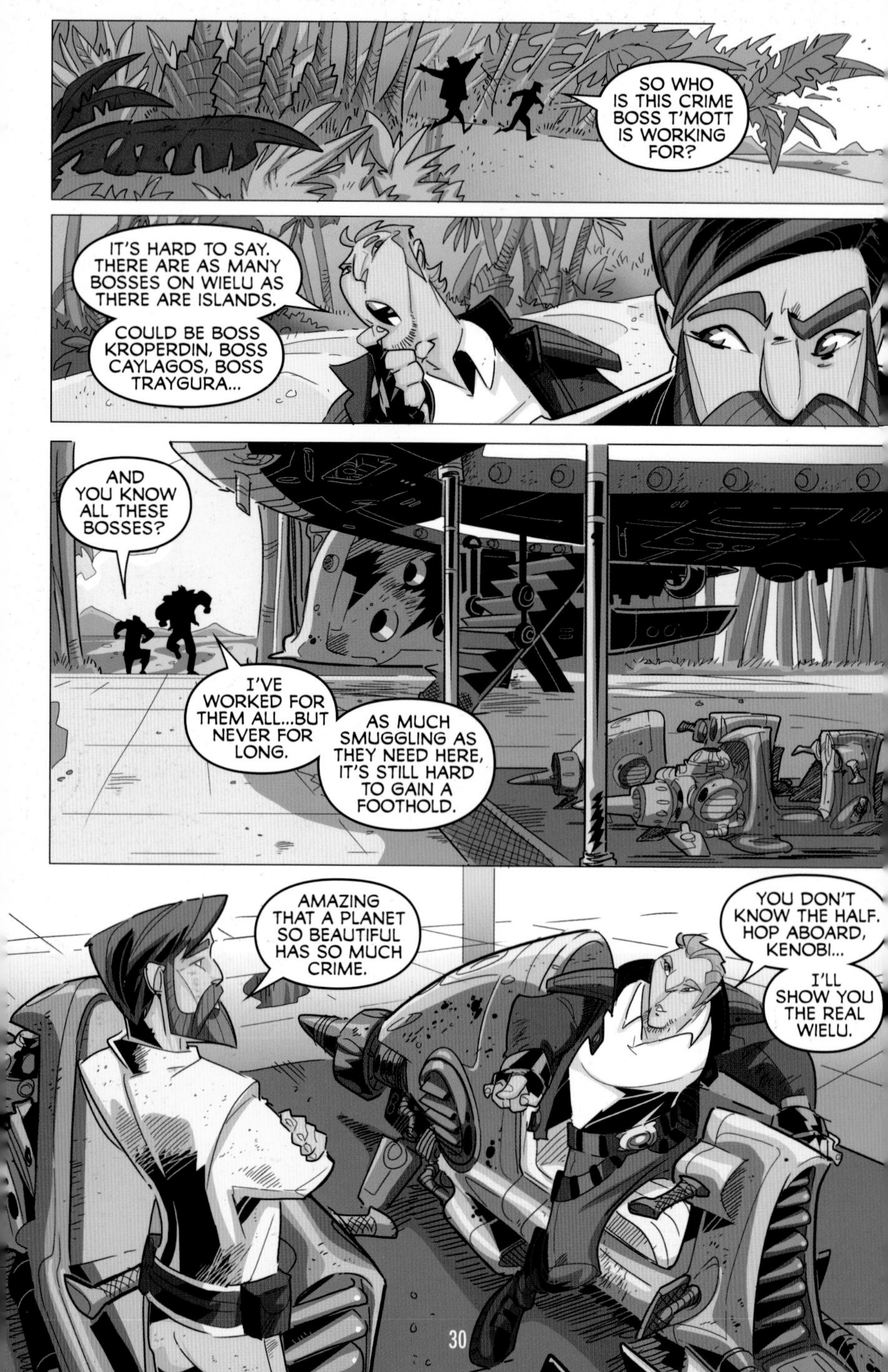

SO WHO IS THIS CRIME BOSS T'MOTT IS WORKING FOR?
IT'S HARD TO SAY. THERE ARE AS MANY BOSSES ON WIELU AS THERE ARE ISLANDS.
COULD BE BOSS KROPERDIN, BOSS CAYLAGOS, BOSS TRAYGURA...
AND YOU KNOW ALL THESE BOSSES?
I'VE WORKED FOR THEM ALL...BUT NEVER FOR LONG.
AS MUCH SMUGGLING AS THEY NEED HERE, IT'S STILL HARD TO GAIN A FOOTHOLD.
AMAZING THAT A PLANET SO BEAUTIFUL HAS SO MUCH CRIME.
YOU DON'T KNOW THE HALF. HOP ABOARD, KENOBI...
I'LL SHOW YOU THE REAL WIELU.

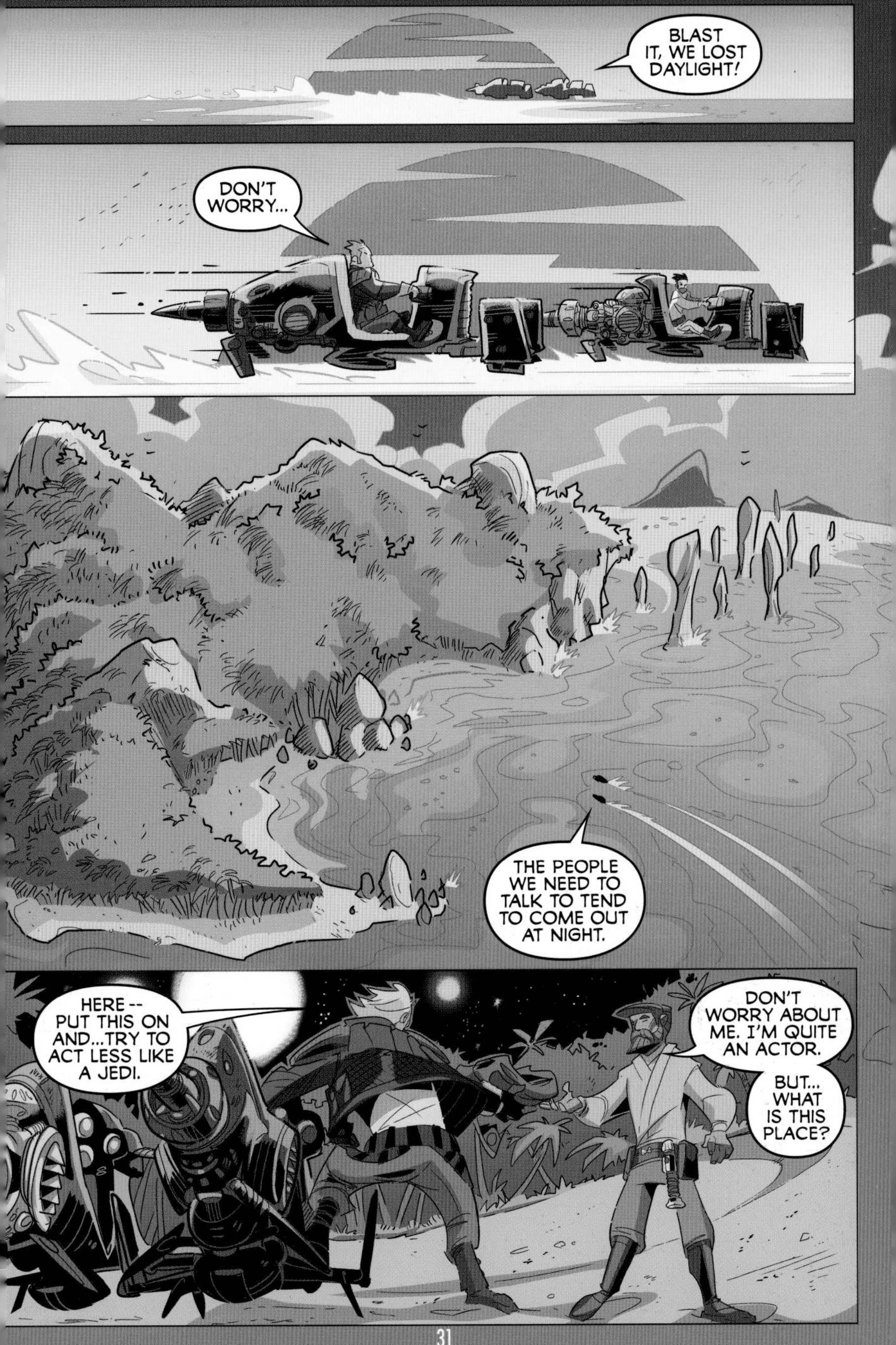
BLAST IT, WE LOST DAYLIGHT!
DON'T WORRY...
THE PEOPLE WE NEED TO TALK TO TEND TO COME OUT AT NIGHT.
HERE -- PUT THIS ON AND...TRY TO ACT LESS LIKE A JEDI.
DON'T WORRY ABOUT ME. I'M QUITE AN ACTOR.
BUT... WHAT IS THIS PLACE?

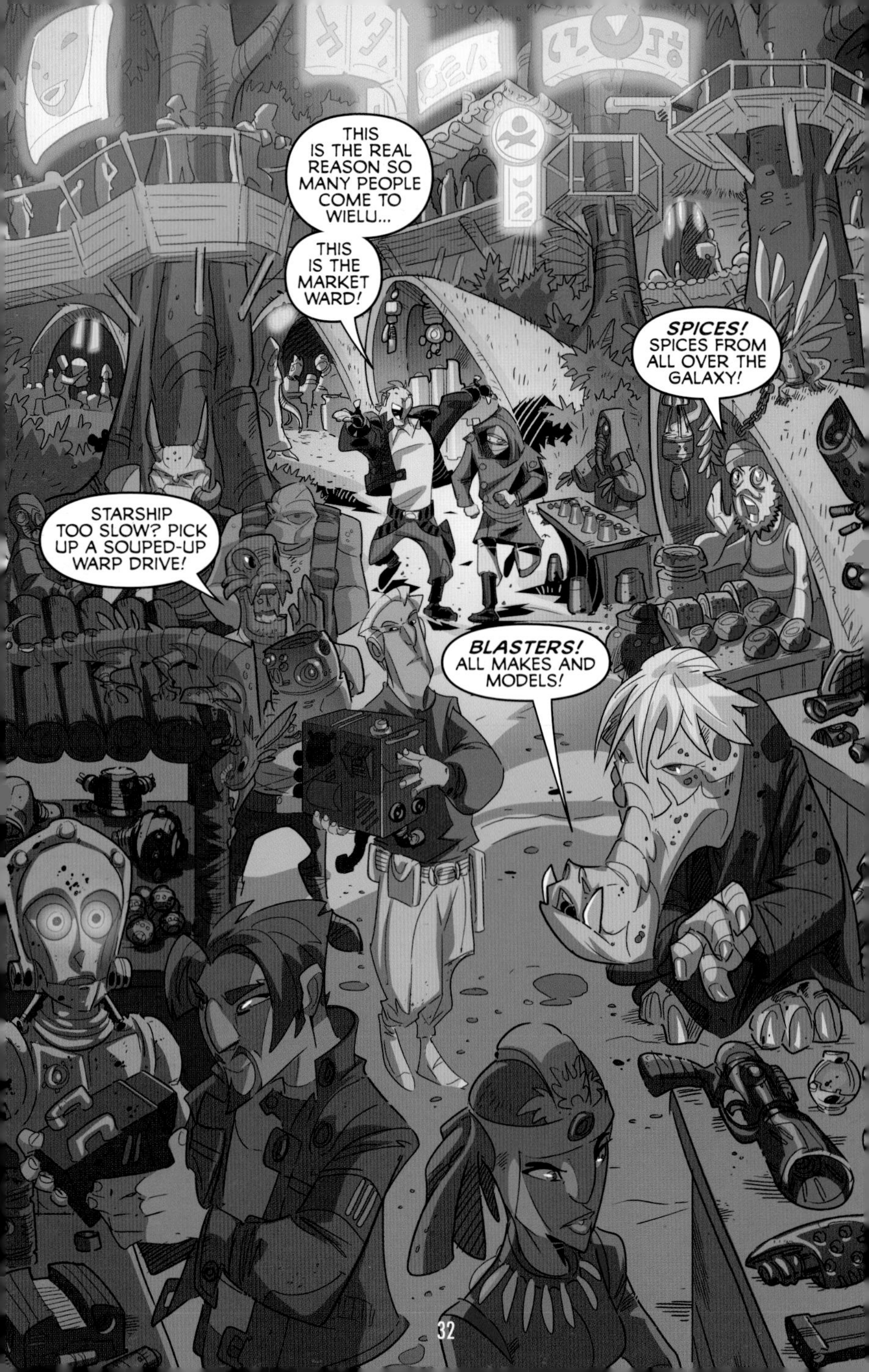
THIS IS THE REAL REASON SO MANY PEOPLE COME TO WIELU...
THIS IS THE MARKET WARD!
SPICES! SPICES FROM ALL OVER THE GALAXY!
STARSHIP TOO SLOW? PICK UP A SOUPED-UP WARP DRIVE!
BLASTERS! ALL MAKES AND MODELS!

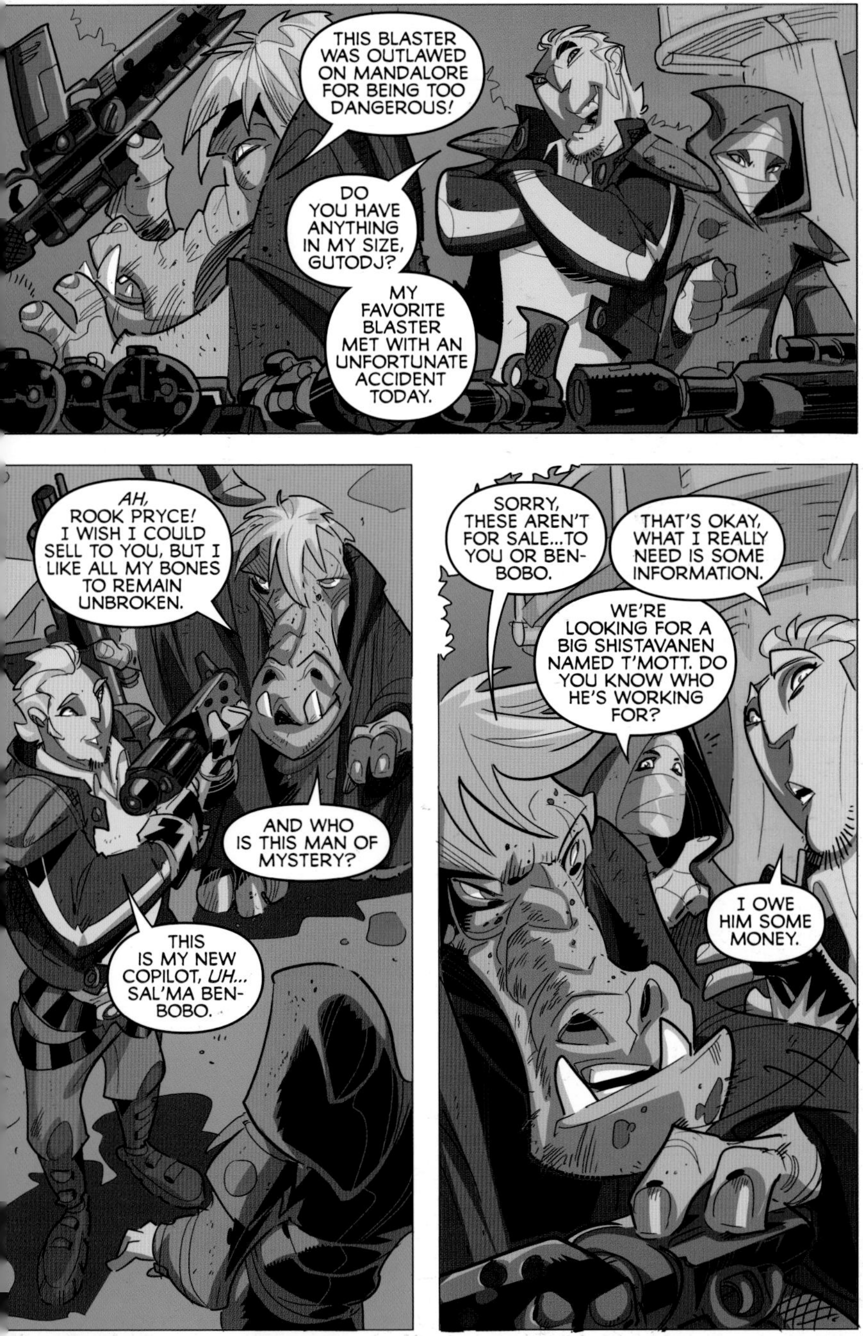
THIS BLASTER WAS OUTLAWED ON MANDALORE FOR BEING TOO DANGEROUS!
DO YOU HAVE ANYTHING IN MY SIZE, GUTODJ?
MY FAVORITE BLASTER MET WITH AN UNFORTUNATE ACCIDENT TODAY.
AH, ROOK PRYCE! I WISH I COULD SELL TO YOU, BUT I LIKE ALL MY BONES TO REMAIN UNBROKEN.
AND WHO IS THIS MAN OF MYSTERY?
THIS IS MY NEW COPILOT, UH... SAL'MA BEN-BOBO.
SORRY, THESE AREN'T FOR SALE...TO YOU OR BEN-BOBO.
THAT'S OKAY, WHAT I REALLY NEED IS SOME INFORMATION.
WE'RE LOOKING FOR A BIG SHISTAVANEN NAMED T'MOTT. DO YOU KNOW WHO HE'S WORKING FOR?
I OWE HIM SOME MONEY.

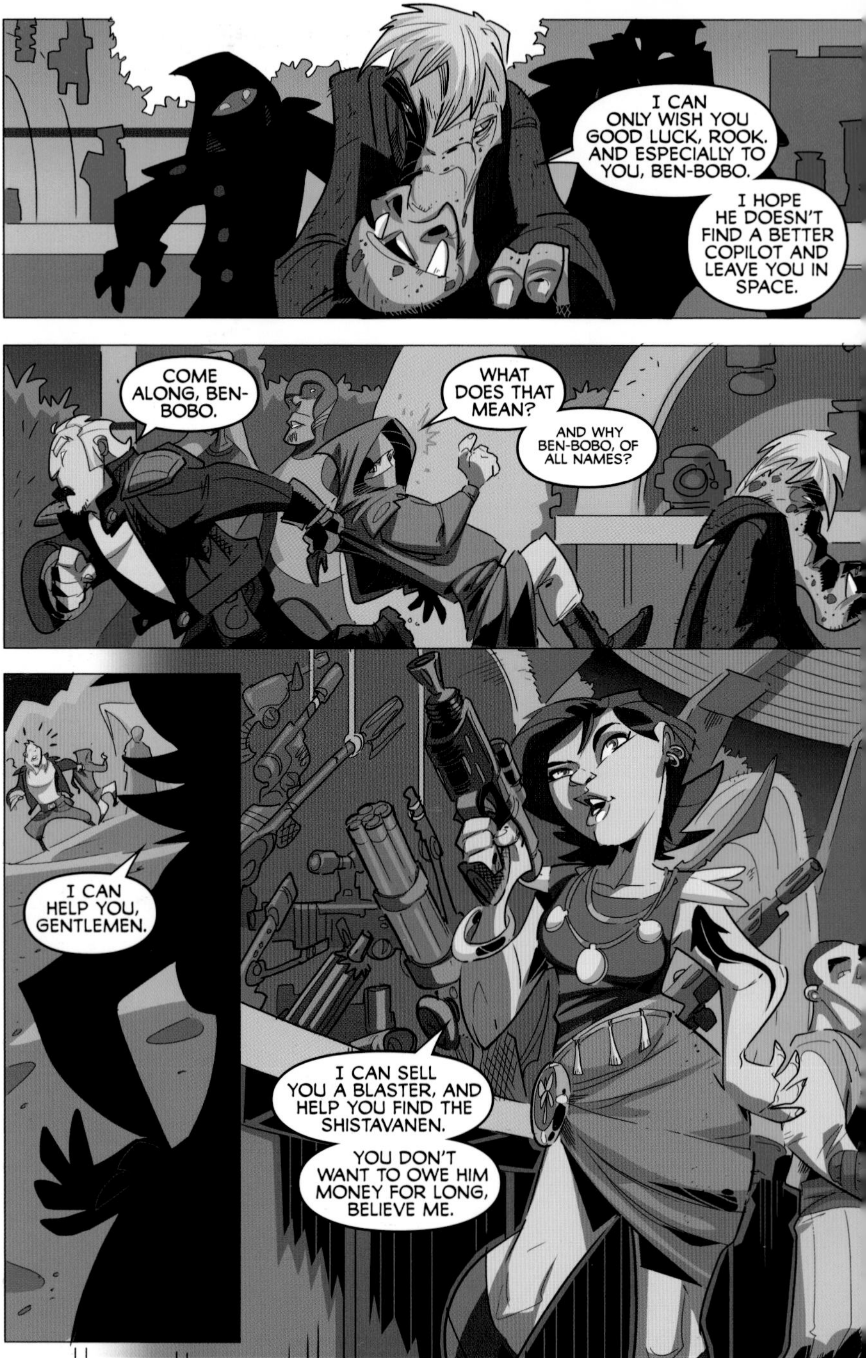
I CAN ONLY WISH YOU GOOD LUCK, ROOK. AND ESPECIALLY TO YOU, BEN-BOBO.
I HOPE HE DOESN'T FIND A BETTER COPILOT AND LEAVE YOU IN SPACE.
COME ALONG, BEN-BOBO.
WHAT DOES THAT MEAN?
AND WHY BEN-BOBO, OF ALL NAMES?
I CAN HELP YOU, GENTLEMEN.
I CAN SELL YOU A BLASTER, AND HELP YOU FIND THE SHISTAVANEN.
YOU DON'T WANT TO OWE HIM MONEY FOR LONG, BELIEVE ME.

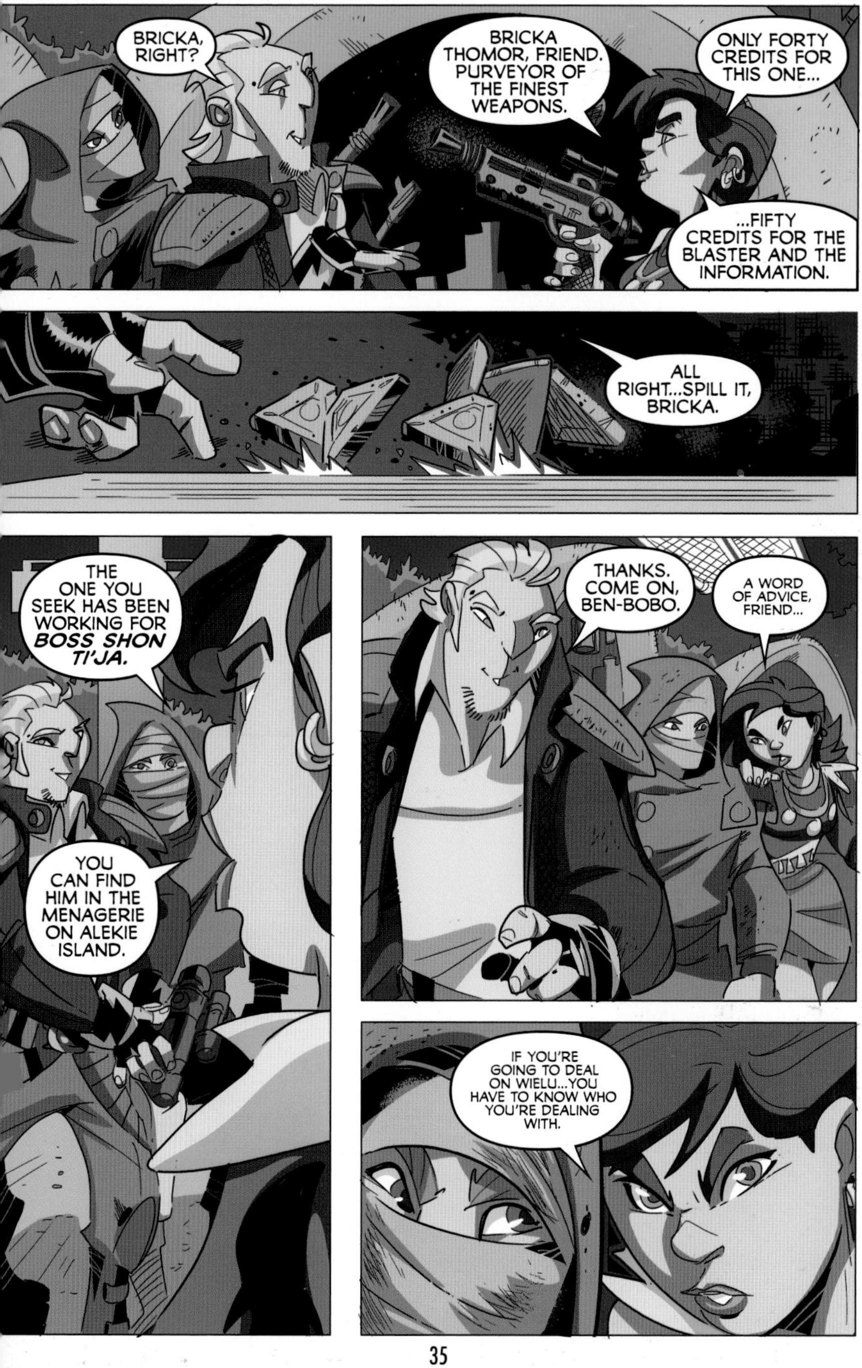
BRICKA, RIGHT?
BRICKA THOMOR, FRIEND. PURVEYOR OF THE FINEST WEAPONS.
ONLY FORTY CREDITS FOR THIS ONE...
...FIFTY CREDITS FOR THE BLASTER AND THE INFORMATION.
ALL RIGHT...SPILL IT, BRICKA.
THE ONE YOU SEEK HAS BEEN WORKING FOR ***BOSS SHON TI'JA.***
YOU CAN FIND HIM IN THE MENAGERIE ON ALEKIE ISLAND.
THANKS. COME ON, BEN-BOBO.
A WORD OF ADVICE, FRIEND...
IF YOU'RE GOING TO DEAL ON WIELU...YOU HAVE TO KNOW WHO YOU'RE DEALING WITH.

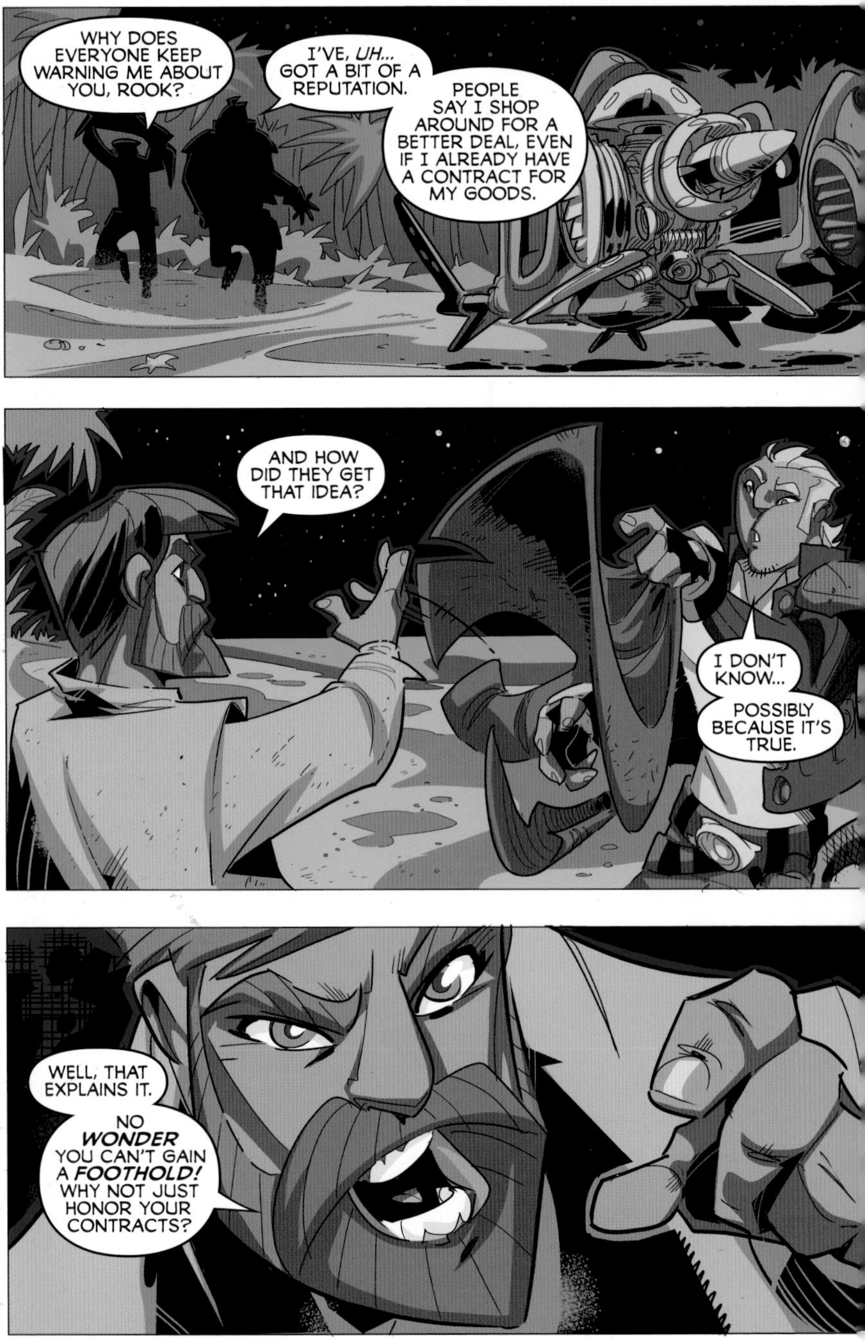
WHY DOES EVERYONE KEEP WARNING ME ABOUT YOU, ROOK?
I'VE, *UH...* GOT A BIT OF A REPUTATION.
PEOPLE SAY I SHOP AROUND FOR A BETTER DEAL, EVEN IF I ALREADY HAVE A CONTRACT FOR MY GOODS.
AND HOW DID THEY GET THAT IDEA?
I DON'T KNOW...
POSSIBLY BECAUSE IT'S TRUE.
WELL, THAT EXPLAINS IT.
NO ***WONDER*** YOU CAN'T GAIN A ***FOOTHOLD!*** WHY NOT JUST HONOR YOUR CONTRACTS?

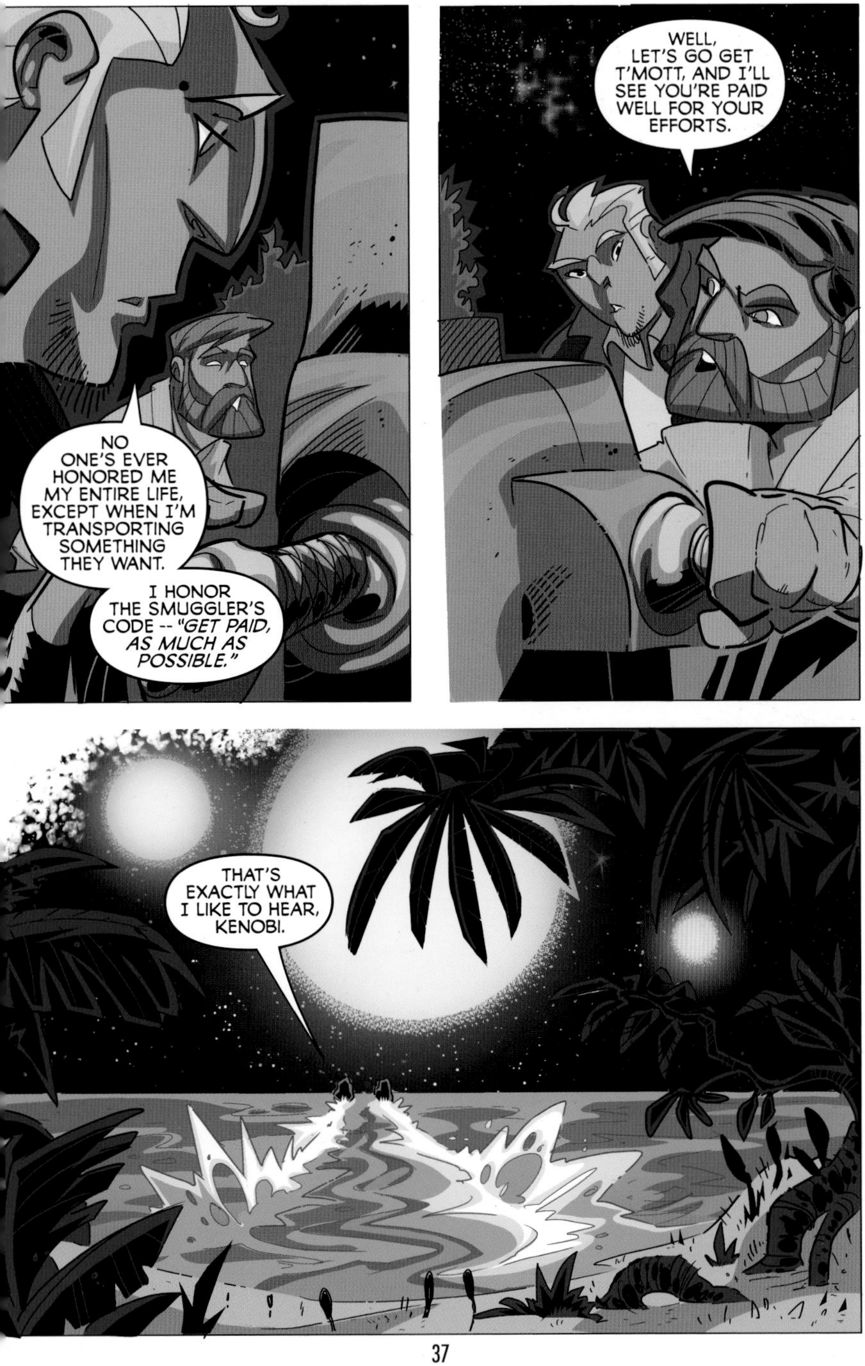
NO ONE'S EVER HONORED ME MY ENTIRE LIFE, EXCEPT WHEN I'M TRANSPORTING SOMETHING THEY WANT.
I HONOR THE SMUGGLER'S CODE -- *"GET PAID, AS MUCH AS POSSIBLE."*
WELL, LET'S GO GET T'MOTT, AND I'LL SEE YOU'RE PAID WELL FOR YOUR EFFORTS.
THAT'S EXACTLY WHAT I LIKE TO HEAR, KENOBI.

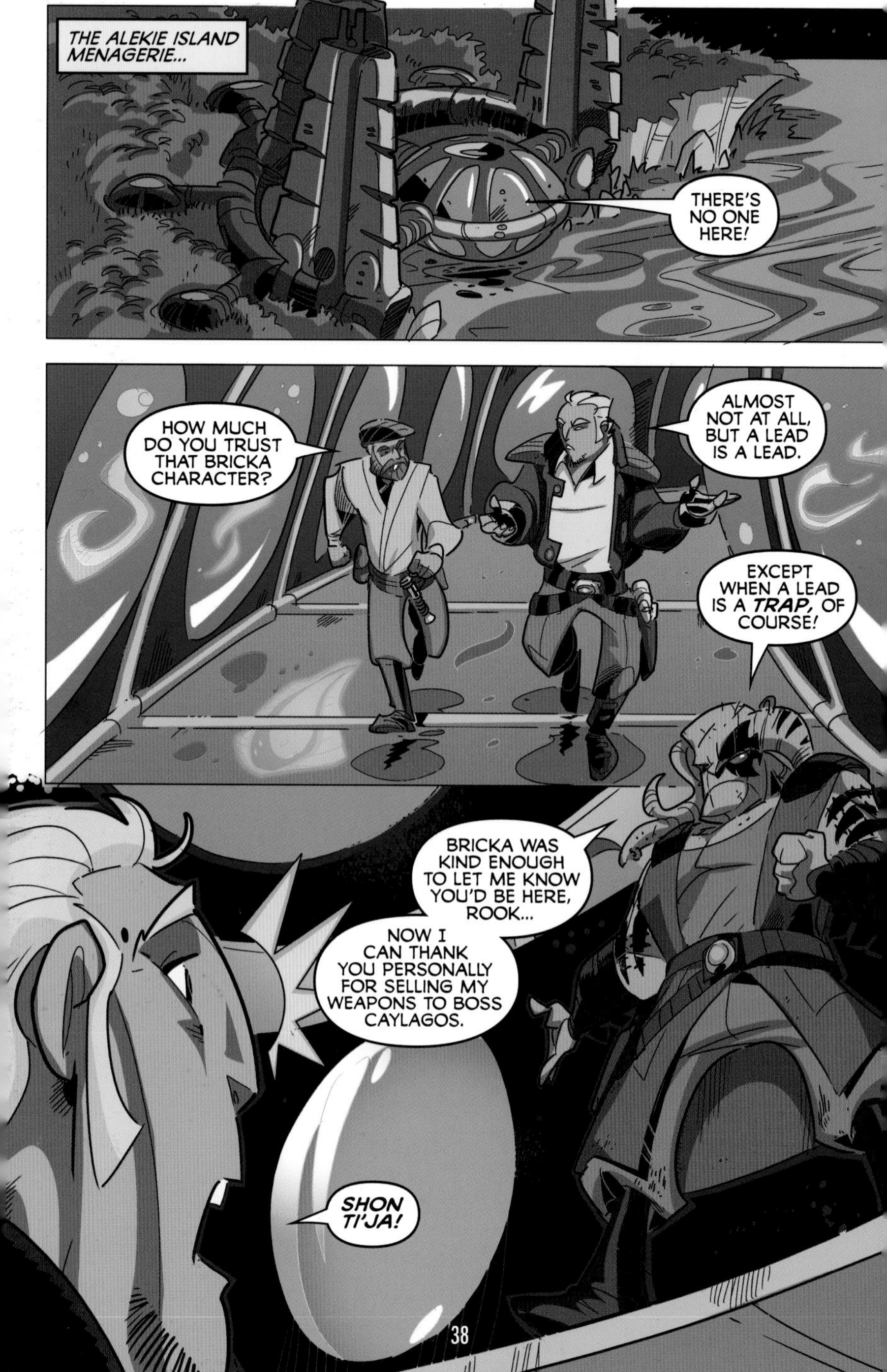
THE ALEKIE ISLAND MENAGERIE...
THERE'S NO ONE HERE!
HOW MUCH DO YOU TRUST THAT BRICKA CHARACTER?
ALMOST NOT AT ALL, BUT A LEAD IS A LEAD.
EXCEPT WHEN A LEAD IS A *TRAP,* OF COURSE!
BRICKA WAS KIND ENOUGH TO LET ME KNOW YOU'D BE HERE, ROOK...
NOW I CAN THANK YOU PERSONALLY FOR SELLING MY WEAPONS TO BOSS CAYLAGOS.
SHON TI'JA!

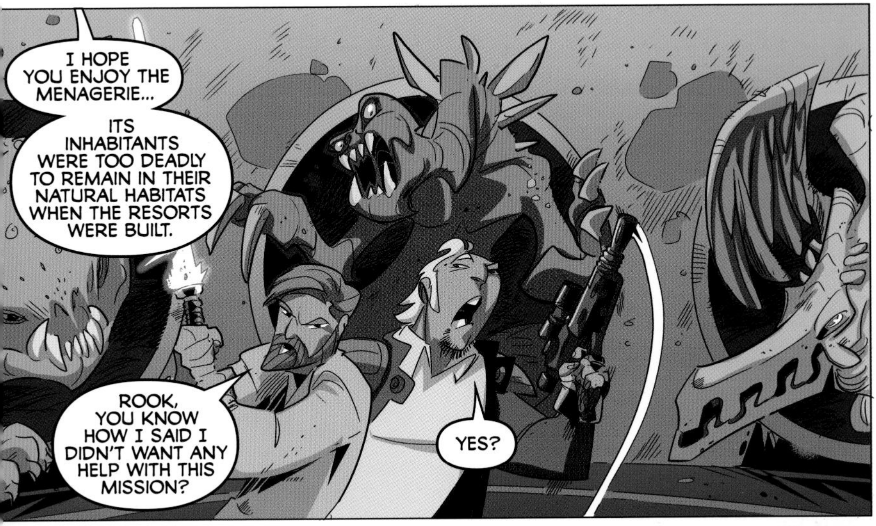
I HOPE YOU ENJOY THE MENAGERIE...
ITS INHABITANTS WERE TOO DEADLY TO REMAIN IN THEIR NATURAL HABITATS WHEN THE RESORTS WERE BUILT.
ROOK, YOU KNOW HOW I SAID I DIDN'T WANT ANY HELP WITH THIS MISSION?
YES?
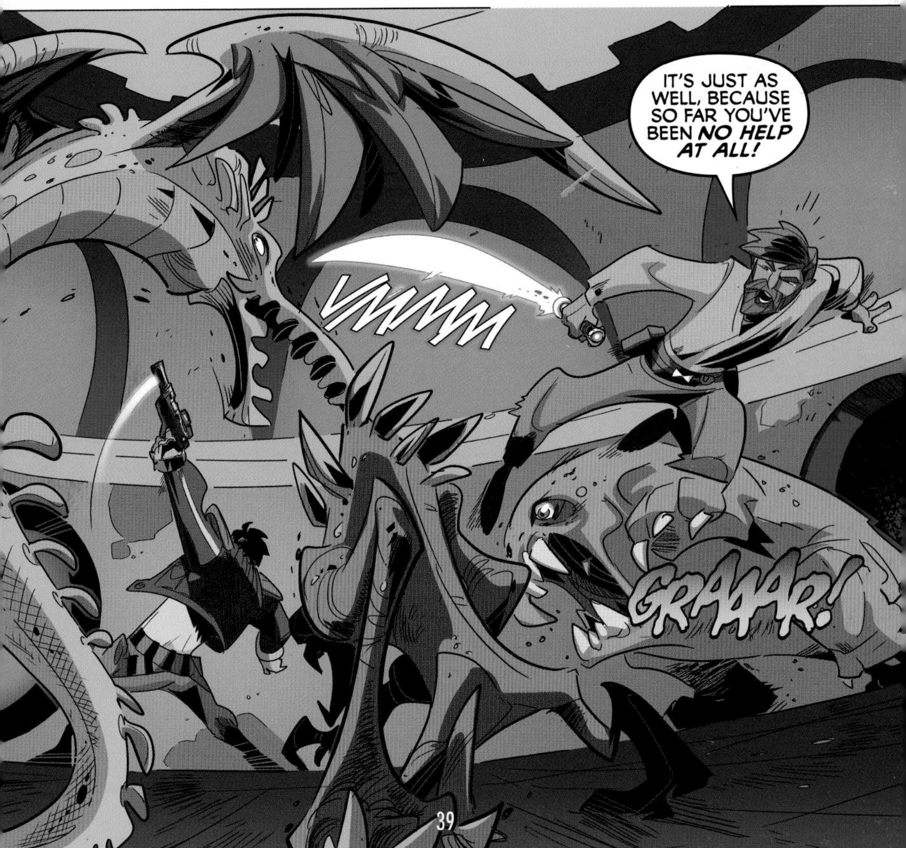
IT'S JUST AS WELL, BECAUSE SO FAR YOU'VE BEEN ***NO HELP AT ALL!***
VMMM
GRAAAR!

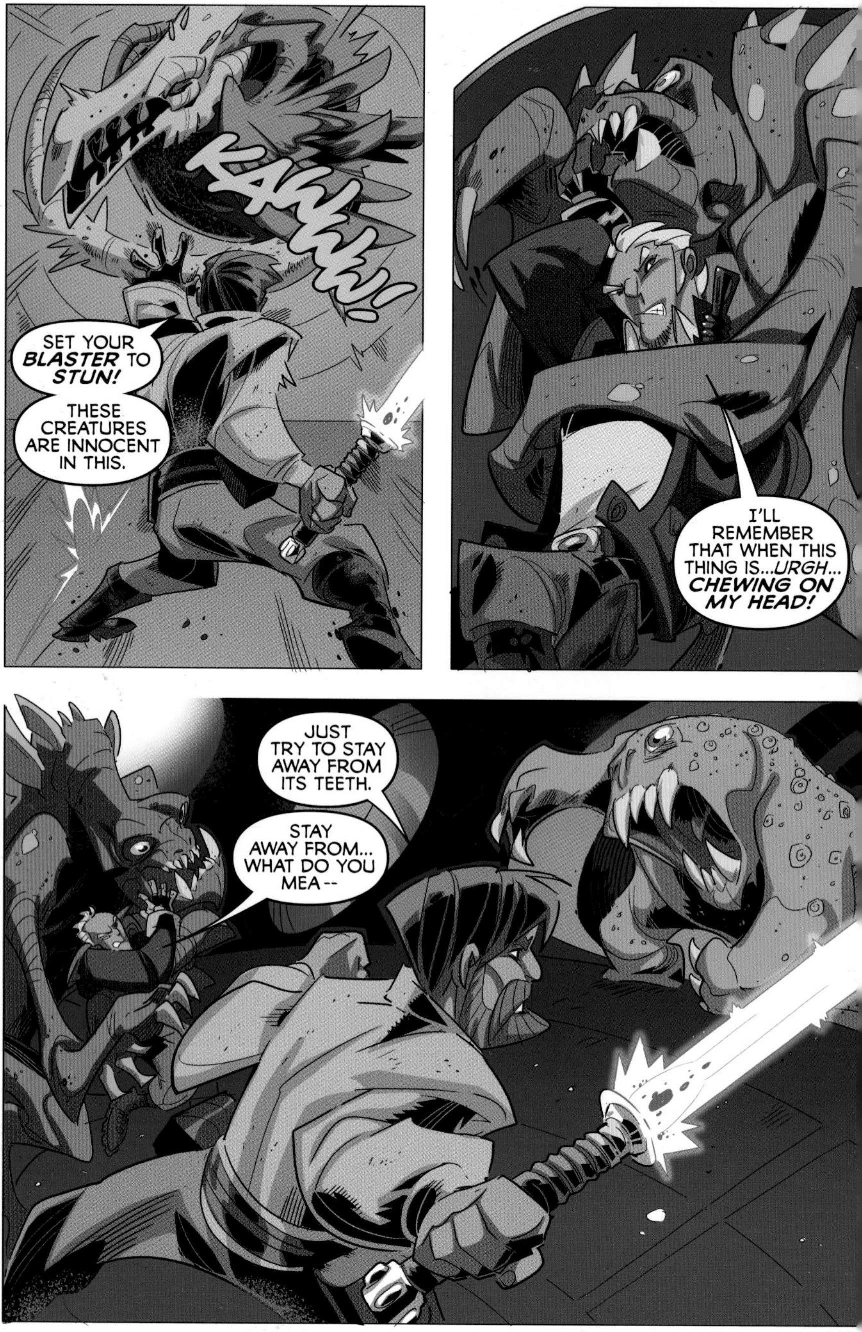
KAWWW!
SET YOUR BLASTER TO STUN!
THESE CREATURES ARE INNOCENT IN THIS.
I'LL REMEMBER THAT WHEN THIS THING IS...URGH... CHEWING ON MY HEAD!
JUST TRY TO STAY AWAY FROM ITS TEETH.
STAY AWAY FROM... WHAT DO YOU MEA--

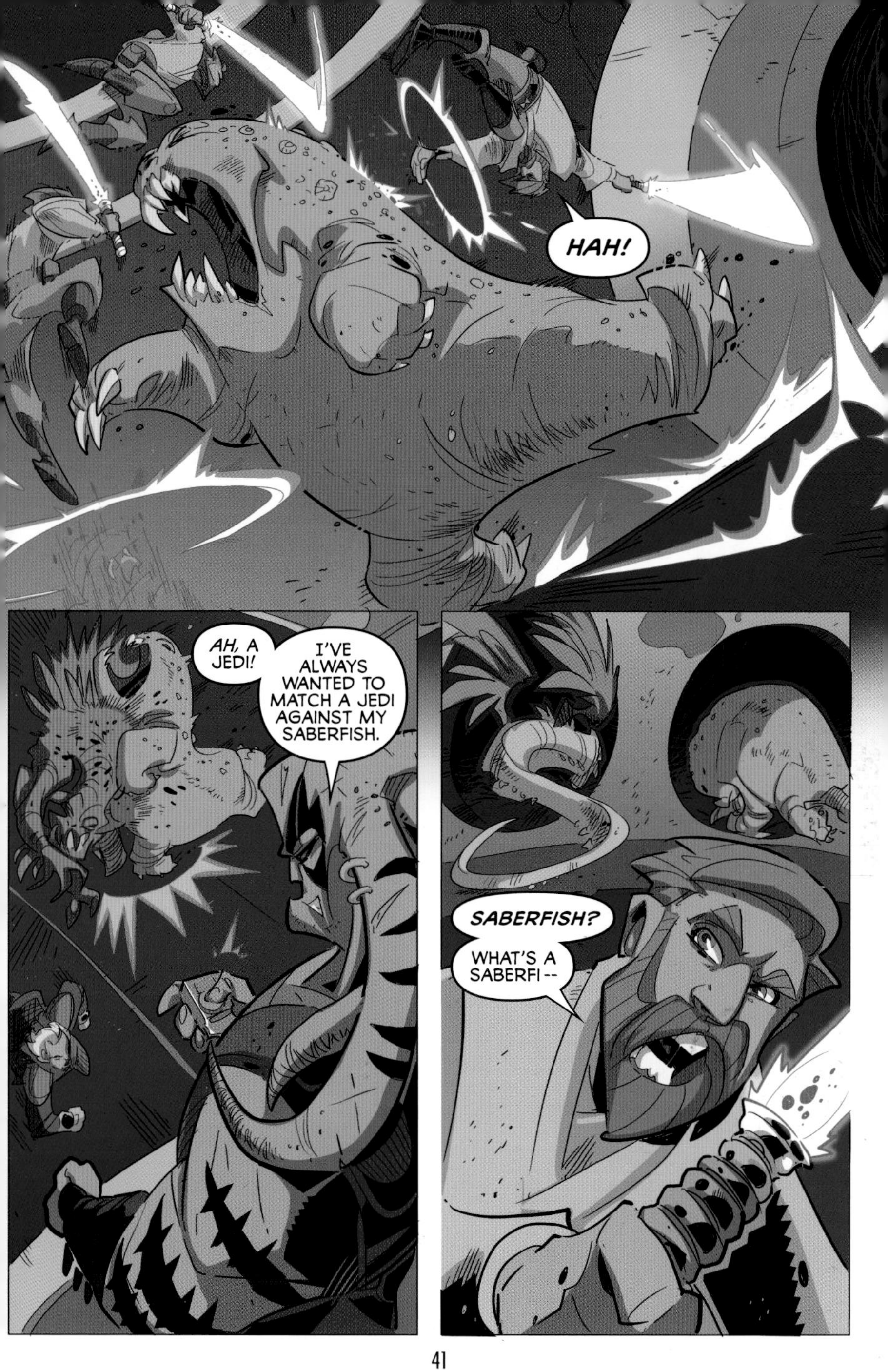
HAH!
AH, A JEDI!
I'VE ALWAYS WANTED TO MATCH A JEDI AGAINST MY SABERFISH.
SABERFISH?
WHAT'S A SABERFI --

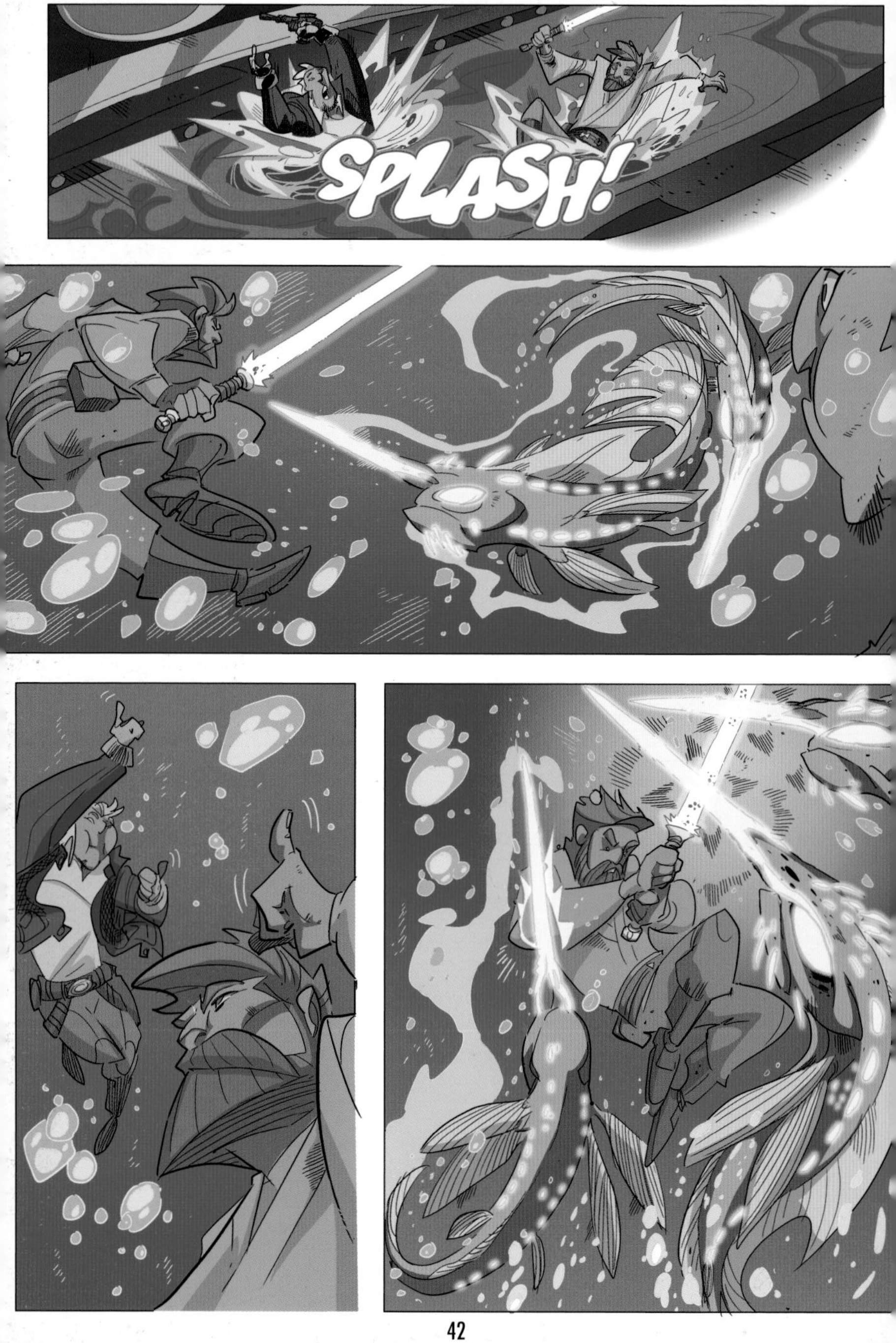
SPLASH!

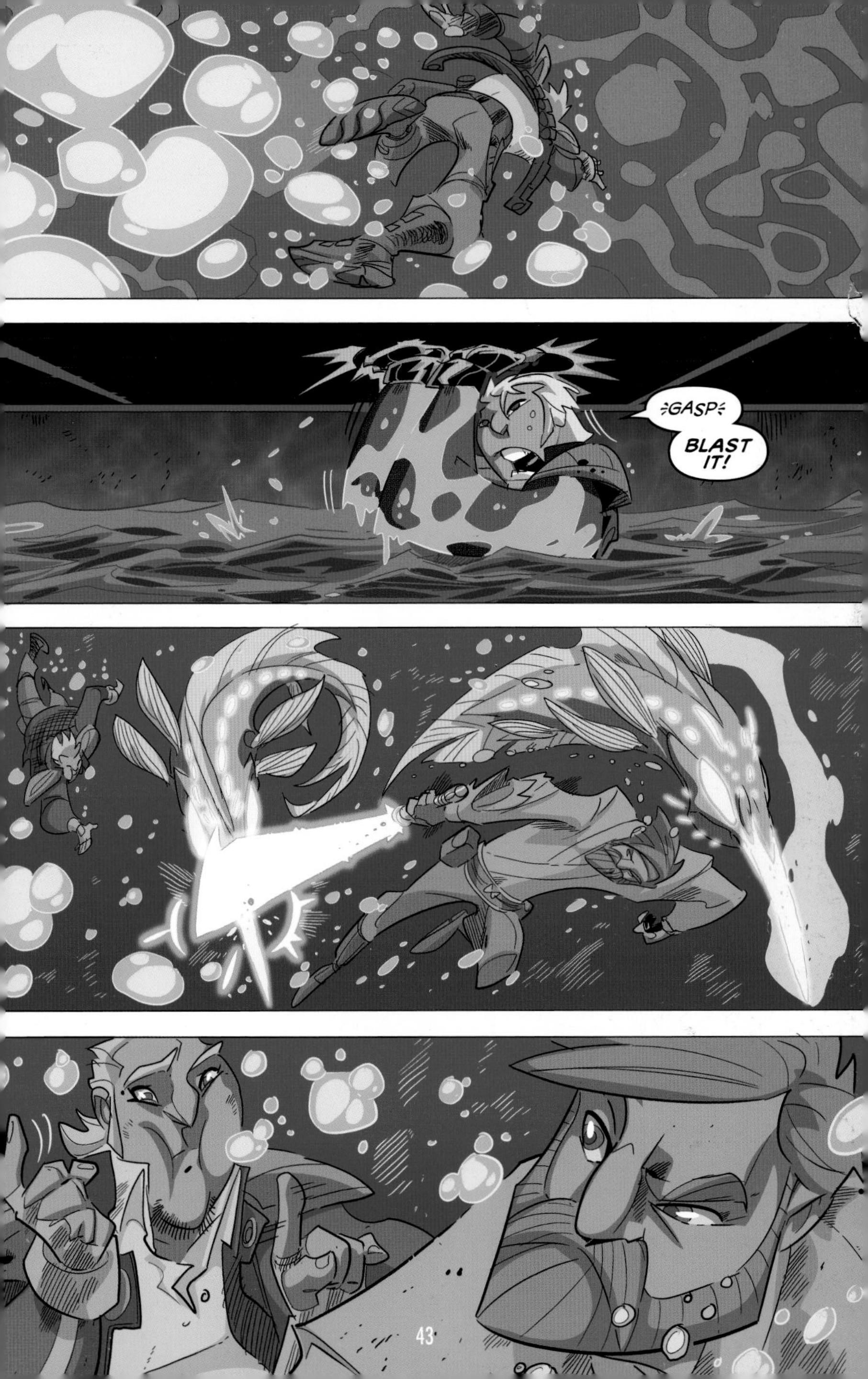
GASP
BLAST IT!

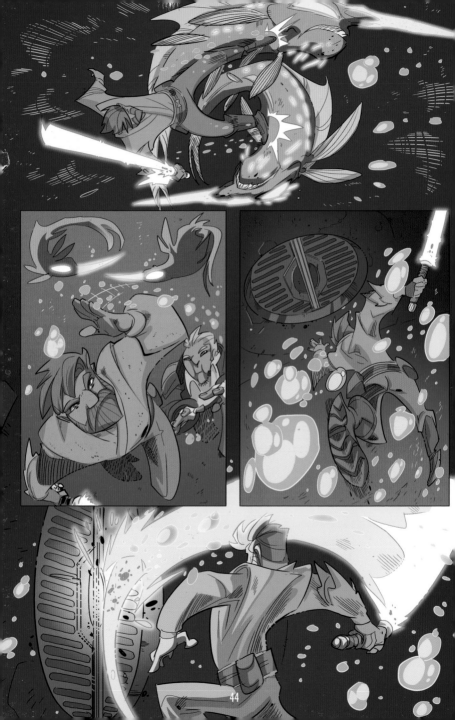

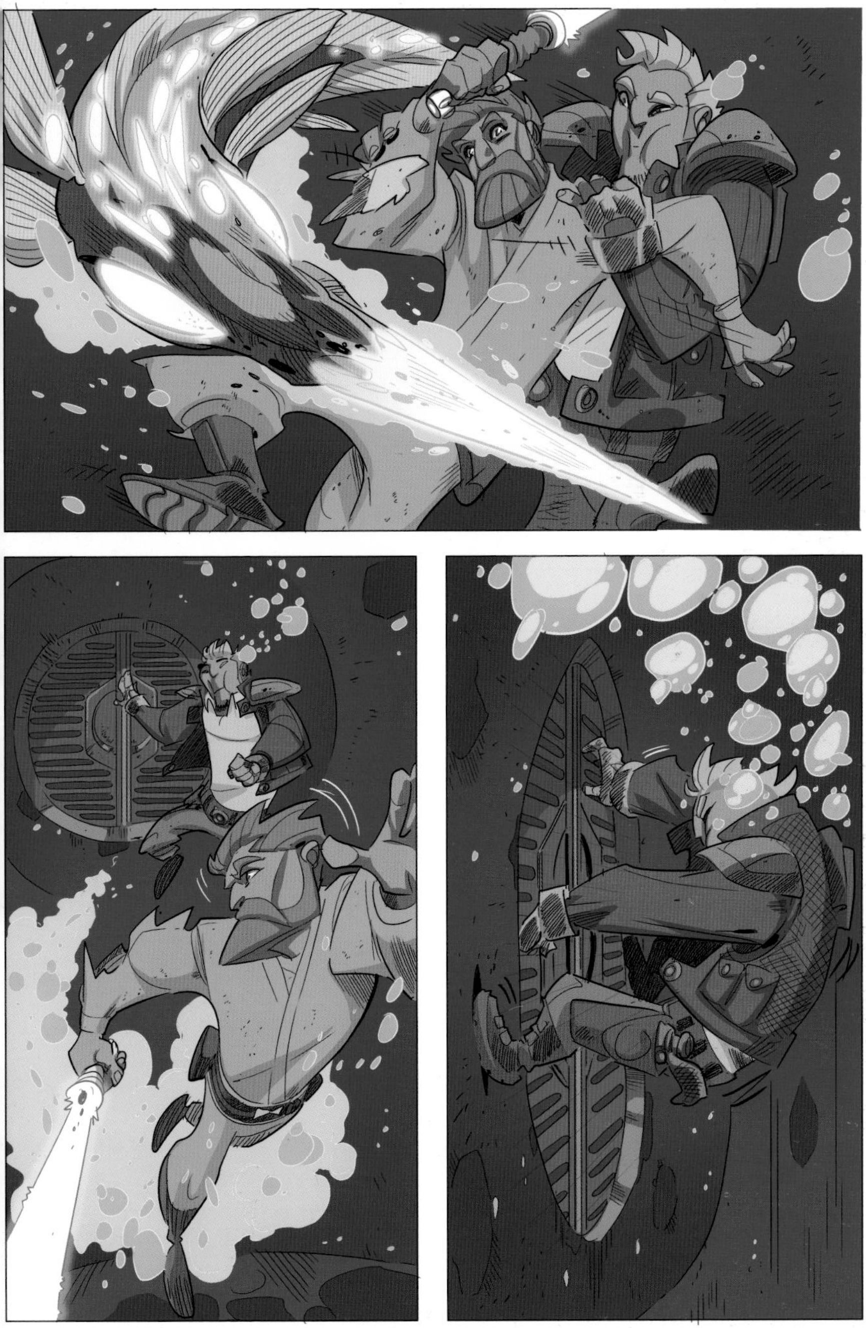

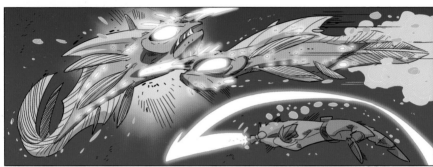

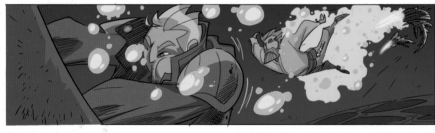

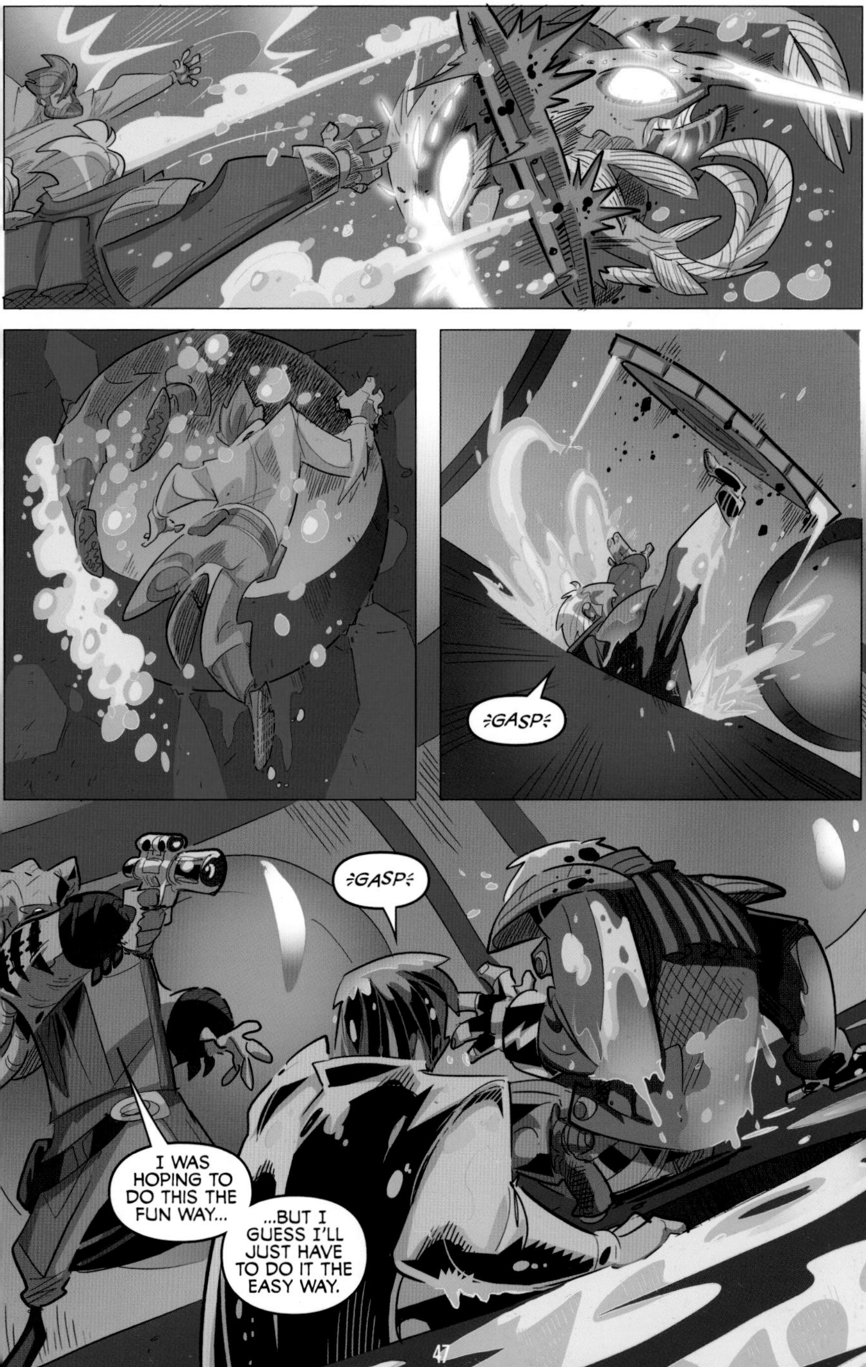
GASP
GASP
I WAS HOPING TO DO THIS THE FUN WAY...
...BUT I GUESS I'LL JUST HAVE TO DO IT THE EASY WAY.

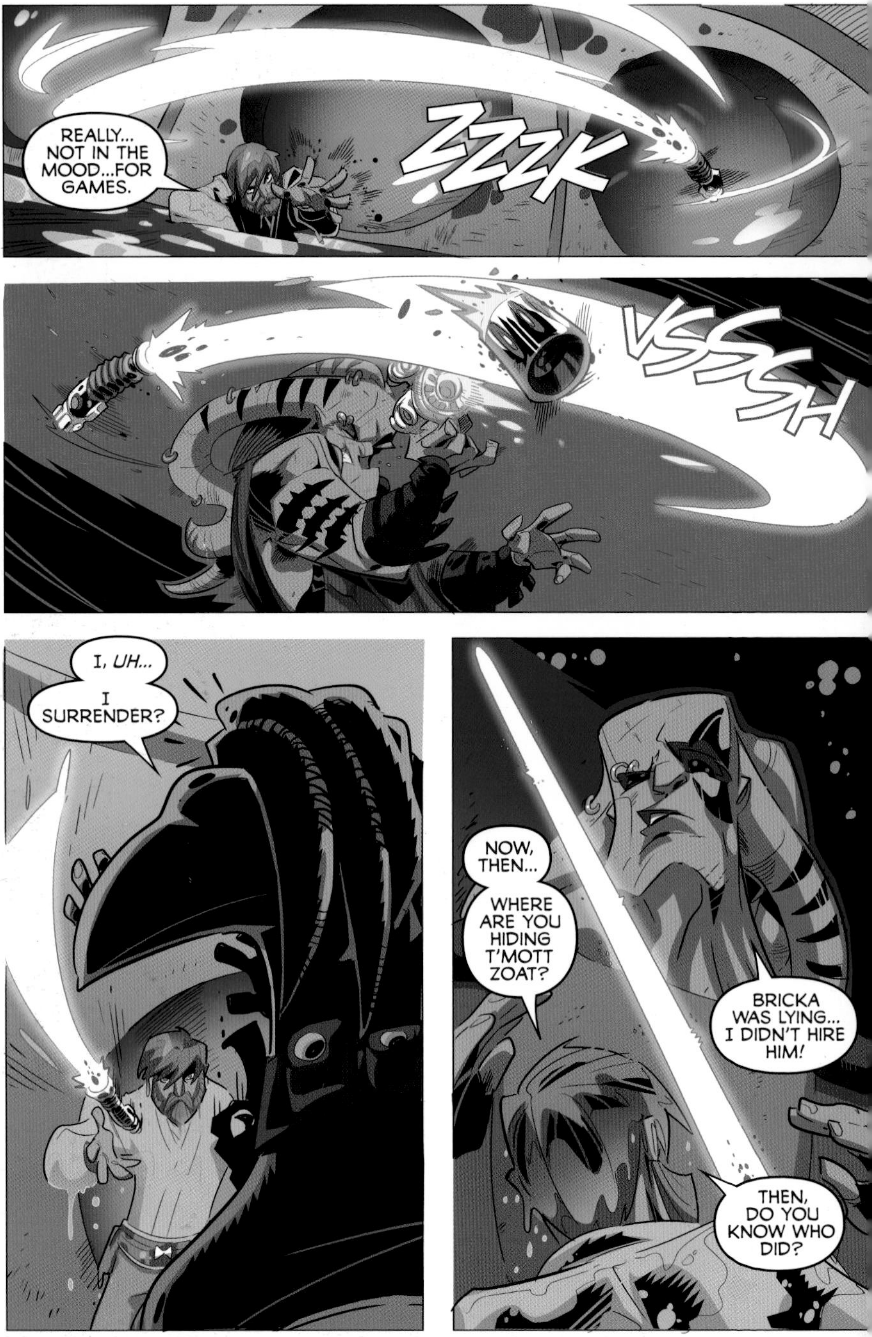
REALLY... NOT IN THE MOOD...FOR GAMES.
ZZZK
VSSSSH
I, UH...
I SURRENDER?
NOW, THEN...
WHERE ARE YOU HIDING T'MOTT ZOAT?
BRICKA WAS LYING... I DIDN'T HIRE HIM!
THEN, DO YOU KNOW WHO DID?

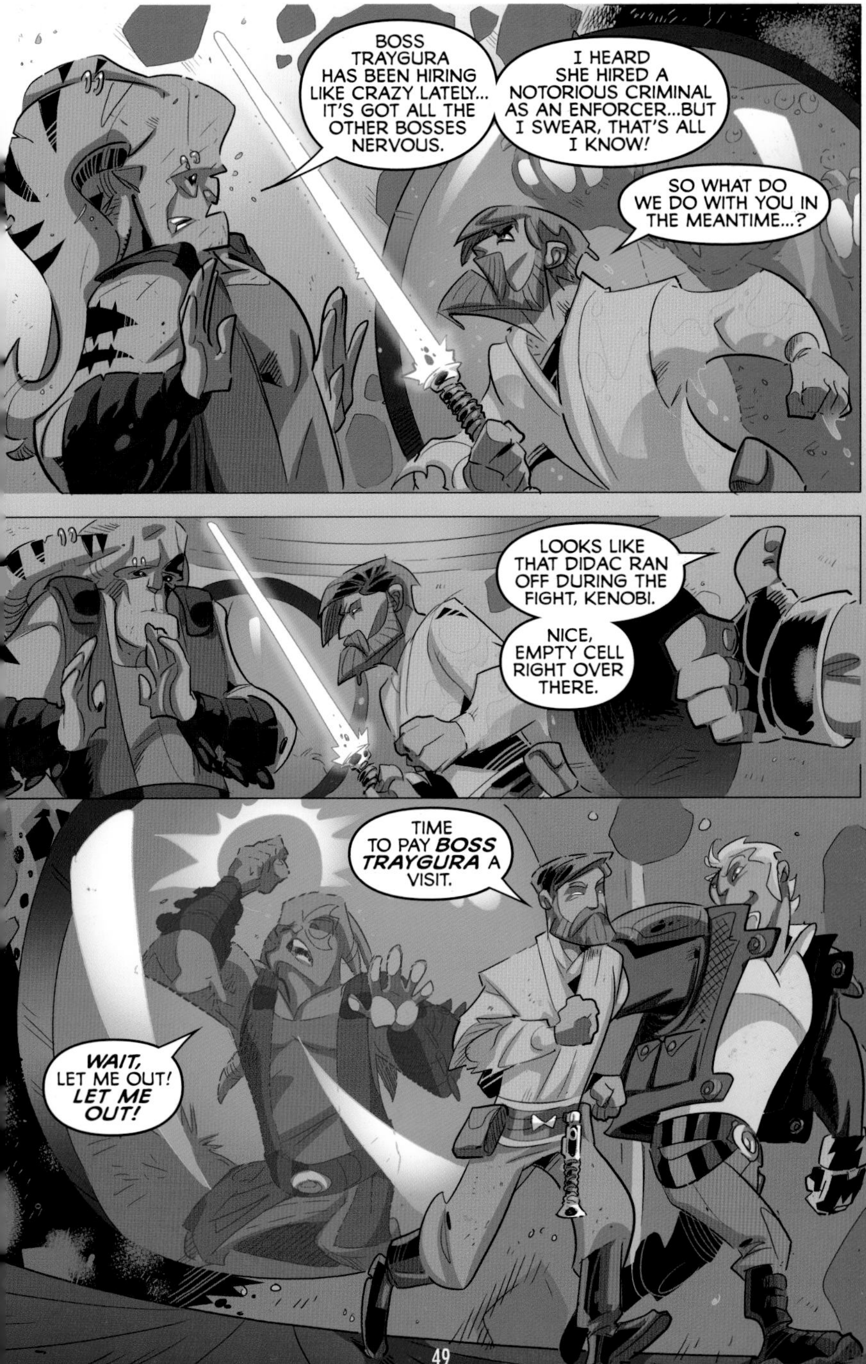
BOSS TRAYGURA HAS BEEN HIRING LIKE CRAZY LATELY... IT'S GOT ALL THE OTHER BOSSES NERVOUS.
I HEARD SHE HIRED A NOTORIOUS CRIMINAL AS AN ENFORCER...BUT I SWEAR, THAT'S ALL I KNOW!
SO WHAT DO WE DO WITH YOU IN THE MEANTIME...?
LOOKS LIKE THAT DIDAC RAN OFF DURING THE FIGHT, KENOBI.
NICE, EMPTY CELL RIGHT OVER THERE.
TIME TO PAY ***BOSS TRAYGURA*** A VISIT.
WAIT, LET ME OUT! ***LET ME OUT!***

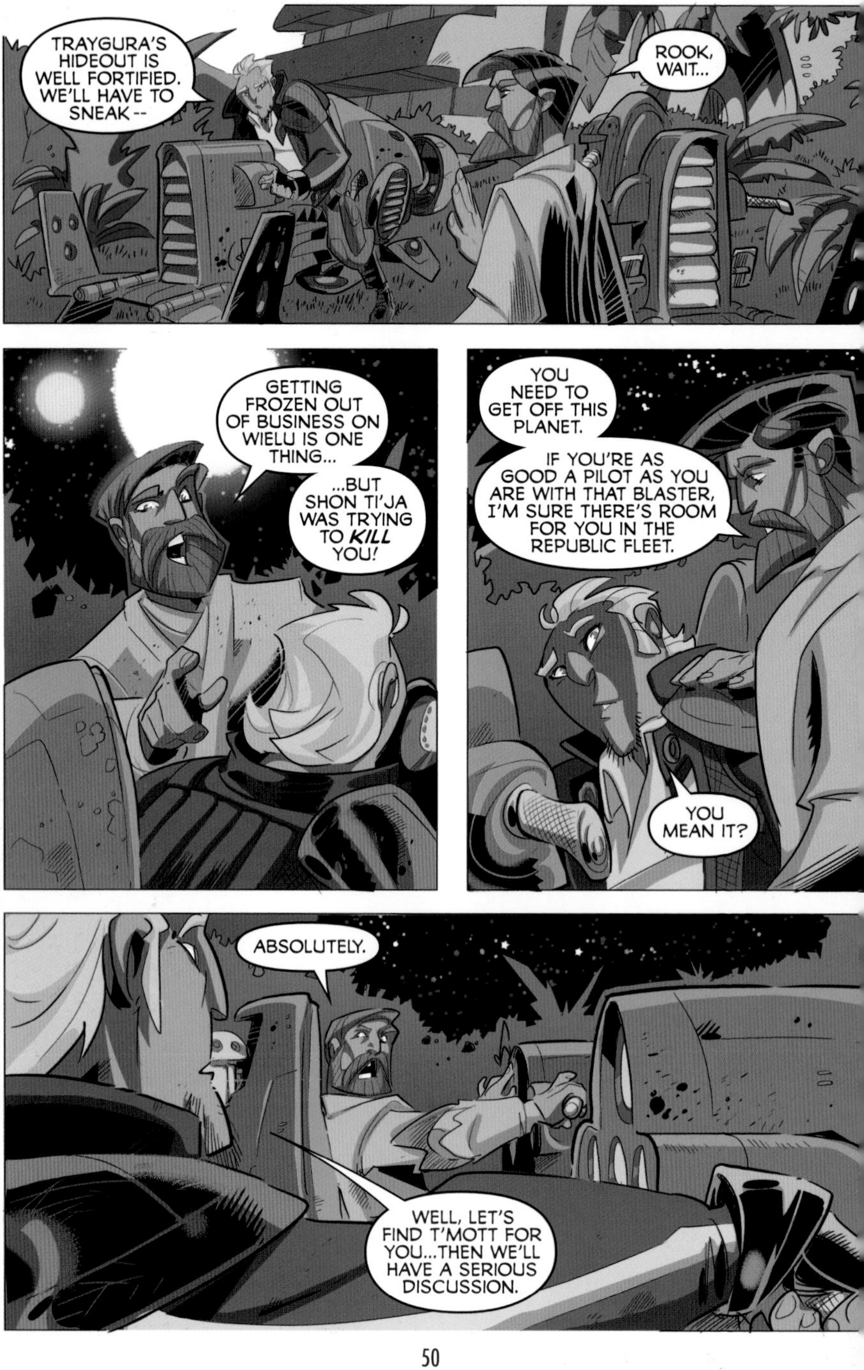
TRAYGURA'S HIDEOUT IS WELL FORTIFIED. WE'LL HAVE TO SNEAK --
ROOK, WAIT...
GETTING FROZEN OUT OF BUSINESS ON WIELU IS ONE THING...
...BUT SHON TI'JA WAS TRYING TO *KILL* YOU!
YOU NEED TO GET OFF THIS PLANET.
IF YOU'RE AS GOOD A PILOT AS YOU ARE WITH THAT BLASTER, I'M SURE THERE'S ROOM FOR YOU IN THE REPUBLIC FLEET.
YOU MEAN IT?
ABSOLUTELY.
WELL, LET'S FIND T'MOTT FOR YOU...THEN WE'LL HAVE A SERIOUS DISCUSSION.

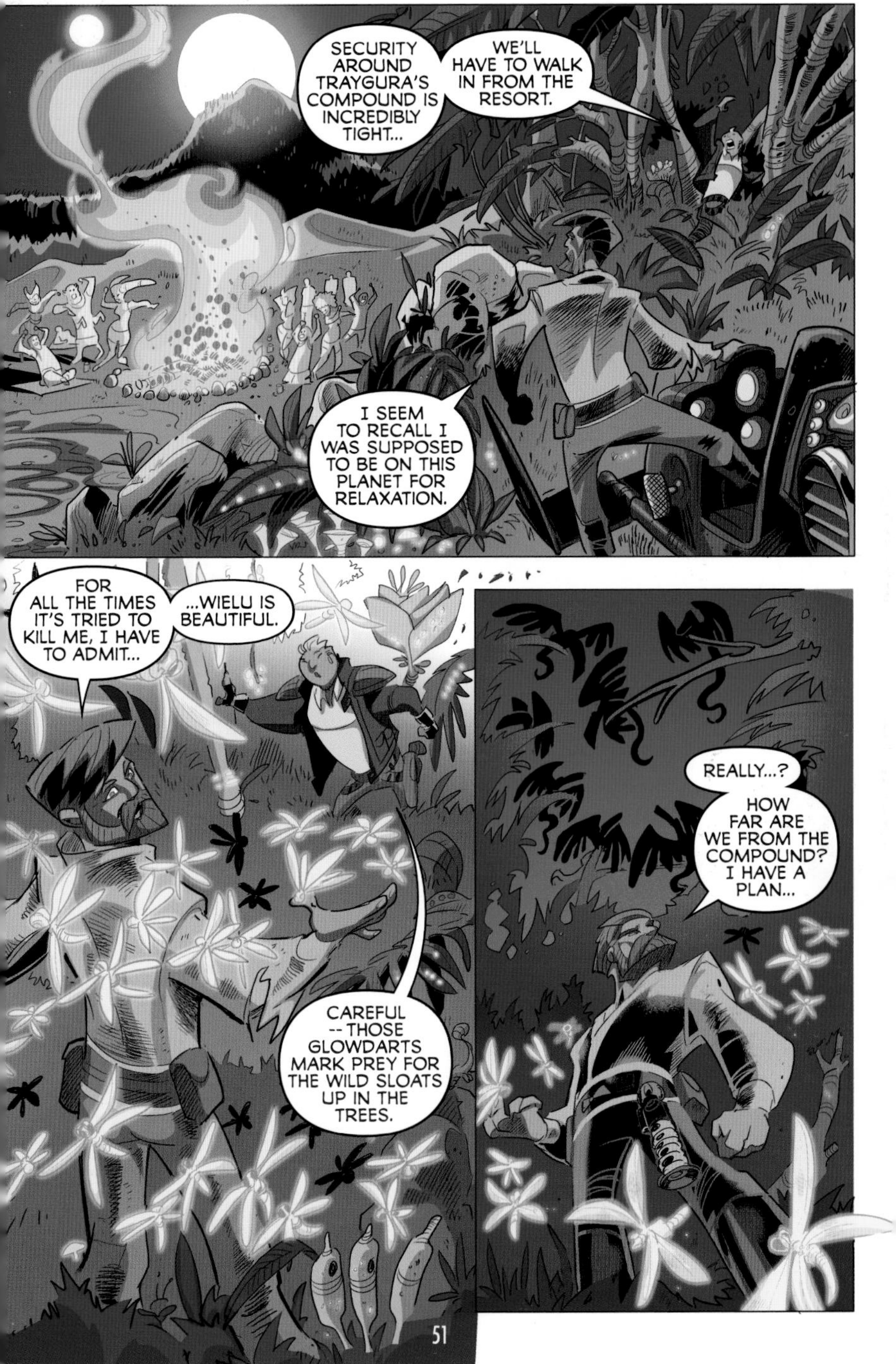
SECURITY AROUND TRAYGURA'S COMPOUND IS INCREDIBLY TIGHT...
WE'LL HAVE TO WALK IN FROM THE RESORT.
I SEEM TO RECALL I WAS SUPPOSED TO BE ON THIS PLANET FOR RELAXATION.
FOR ALL THE TIMES IT'S TRIED TO KILL ME, I HAVE TO ADMIT...
...WIELU IS BEAUTIFUL.
CAREFUL -- THOSE GLOWDARTS MARK PREY FOR THE WILD SLOATS UP IN THE TREES.
REALLY...?
HOW FAR ARE WE FROM THE COMPOUND? I HAVE A PLAN...

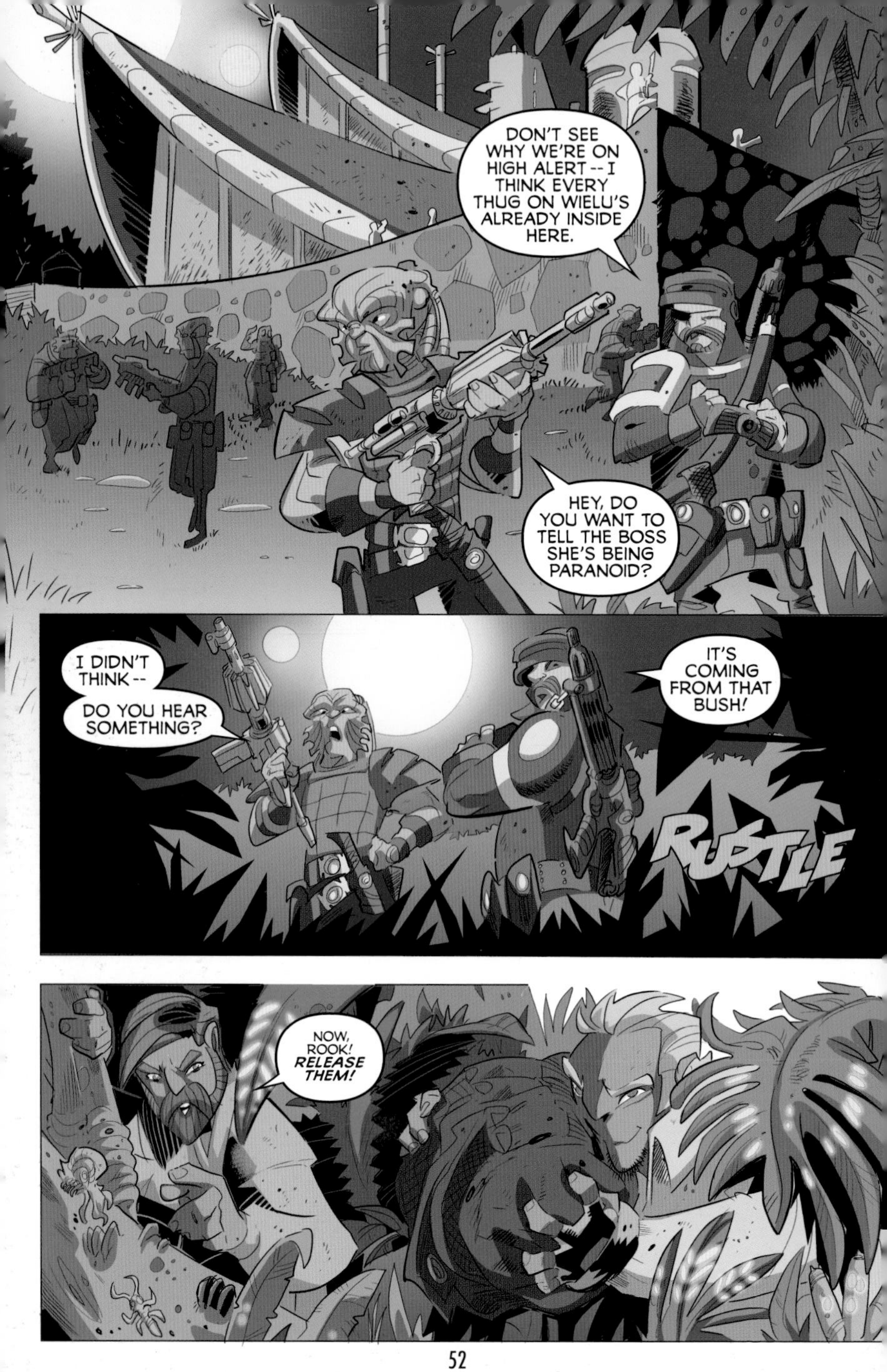
DON'T SEE WHY WE'RE ON HIGH ALERT -- I THINK EVERY THUG ON WIELU'S ALREADY INSIDE HERE.
HEY, DO YOU WANT TO TELL THE BOSS SHE'S BEING PARANOID?
I DIDN'T THINK --
DO YOU HEAR SOMETHING?
IT'S COMING FROM THAT BUSH!
RUSTLE
NOW, ROOK! *RELEASE THEM!*

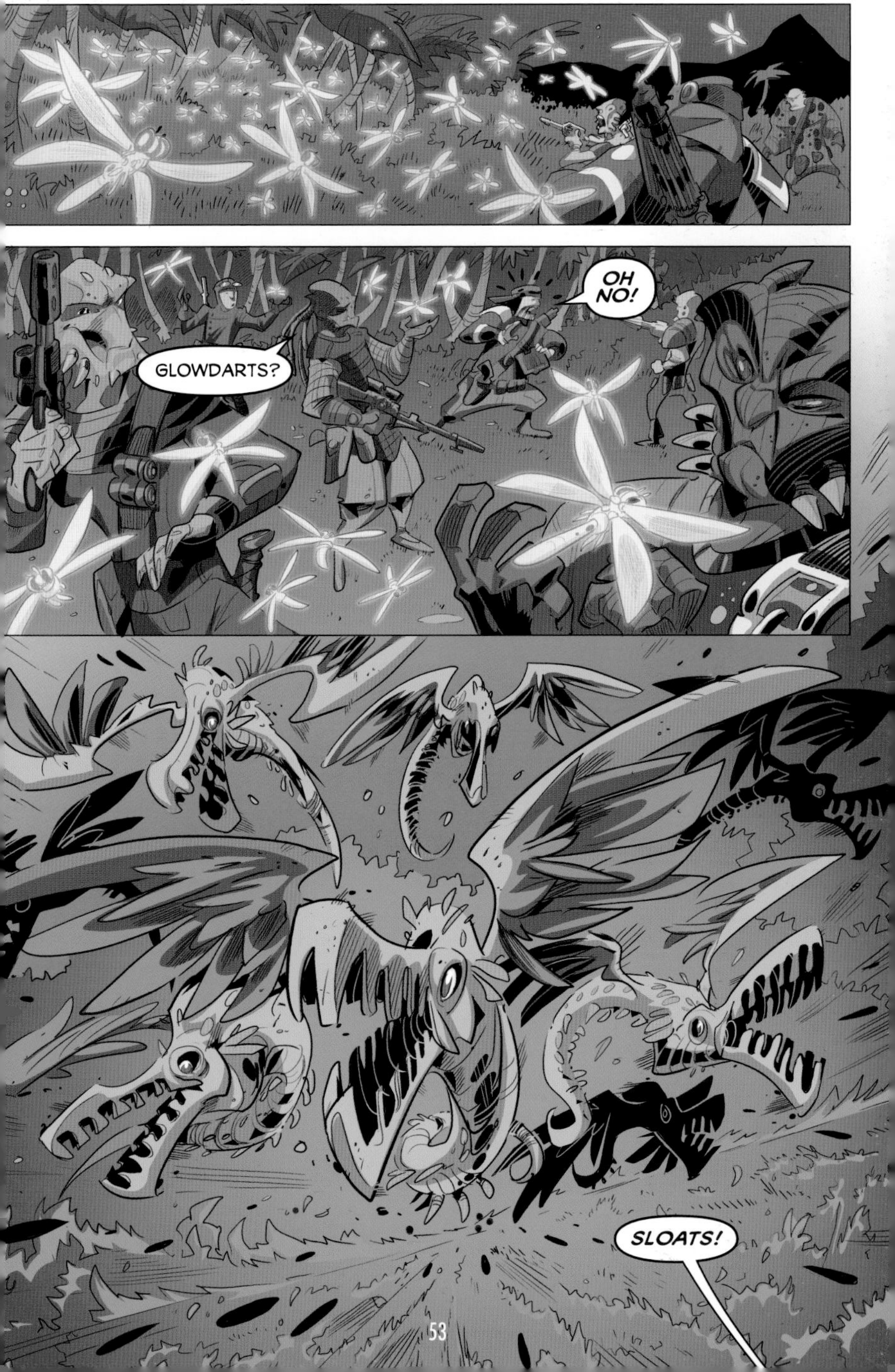
GLOWDARTS?
OH NO!
SLOATS!

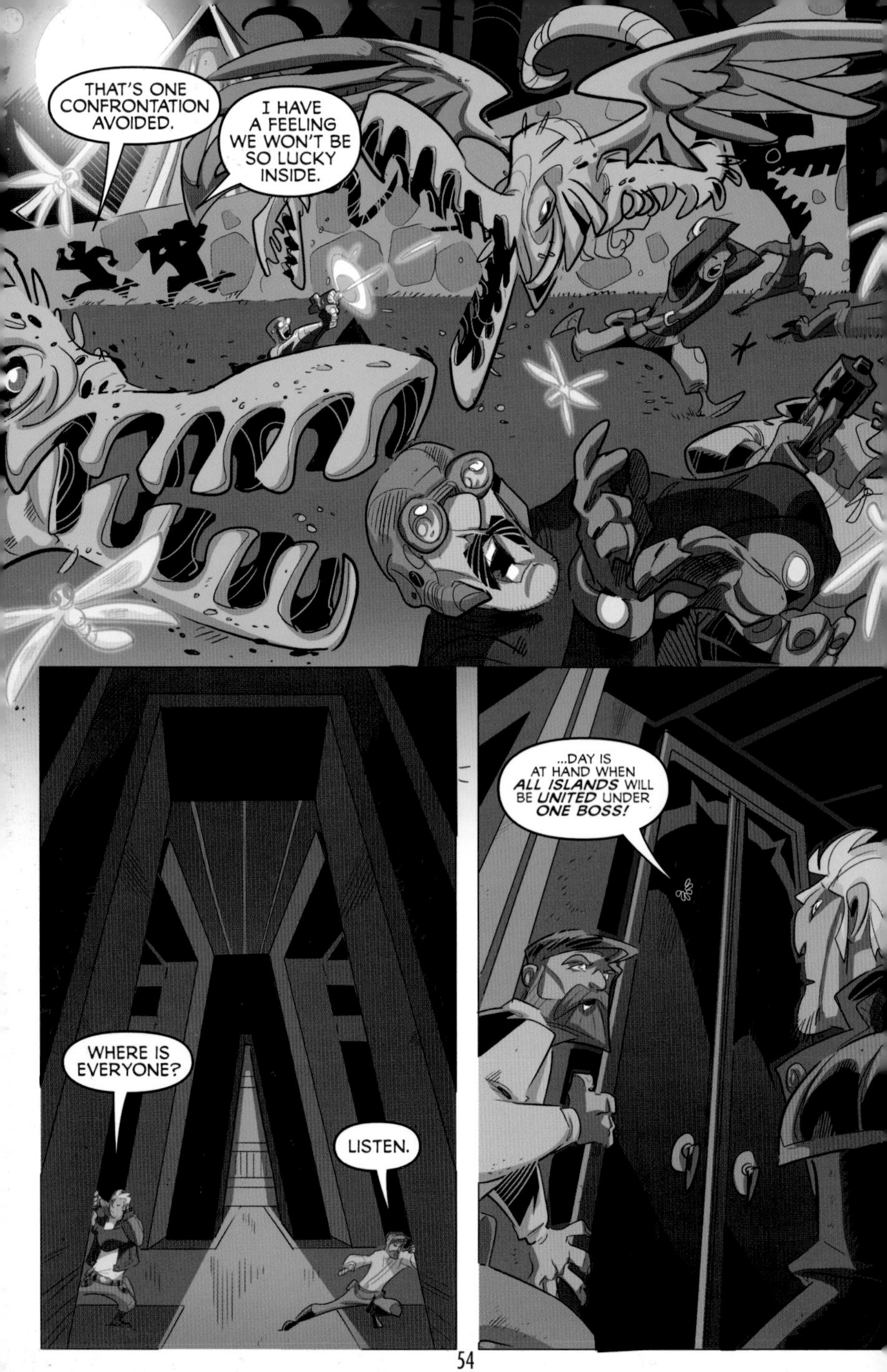
THAT'S ONE CONFRONTATION AVOIDED.
I HAVE A FEELING WE WON'T BE SO LUCKY INSIDE.
WHERE IS EVERYONE?
LISTEN.
...DAY IS AT HAND WHEN ALL ISLANDS WILL BE UNITED UNDER ONE BOSS!

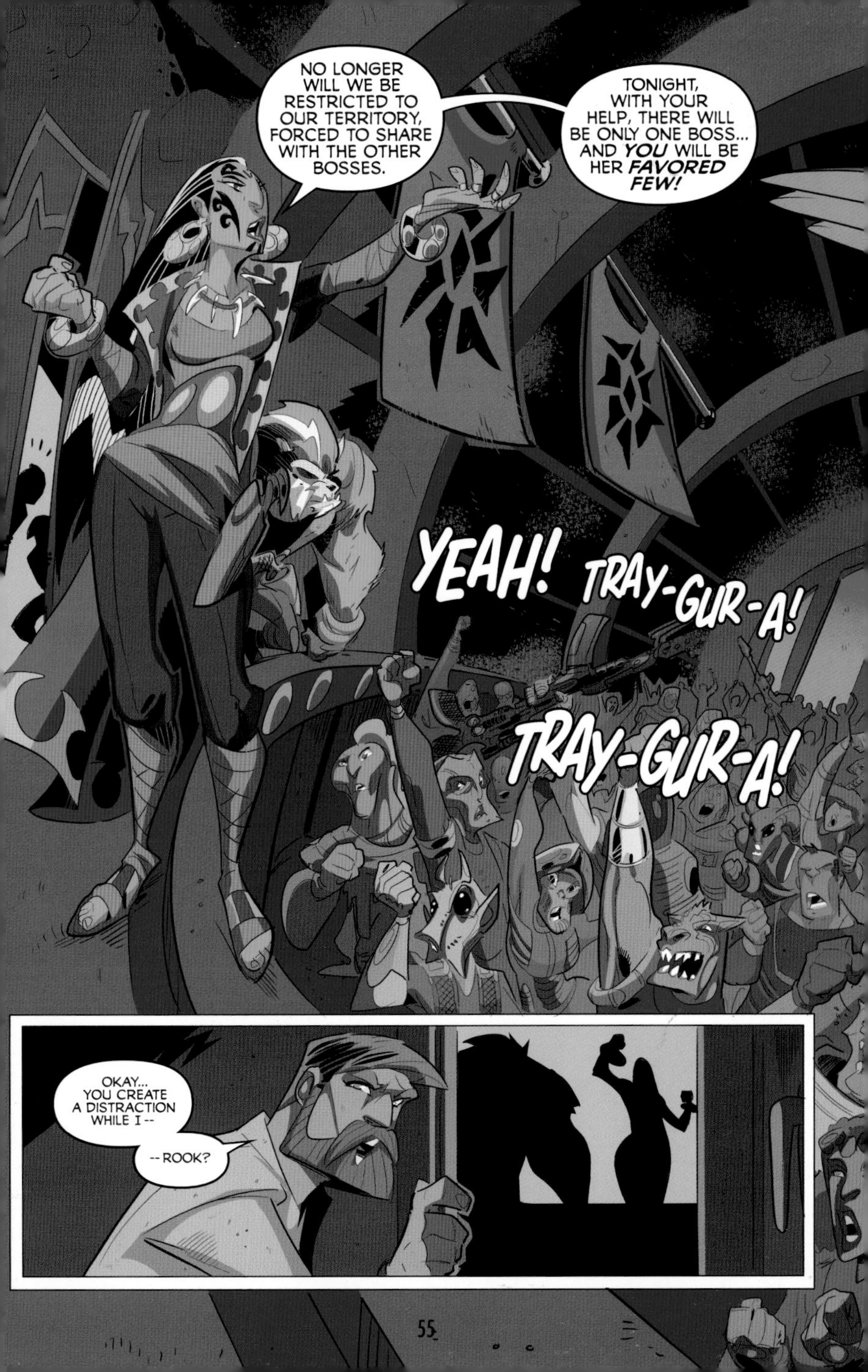
NO LONGER WILL WE BE RESTRICTED TO OUR TERRITORY, FORCED TO SHARE WITH THE OTHER BOSSES.
TONIGHT, WITH YOUR HELP, THERE WILL BE ONLY ONE BOSS... AND YOU WILL BE HER FAVORED FEW!
YEAH!
TRAY-GUR-A!
TRAY-GUR-A!
OKAY... YOU CREATE A DISTRACTION WHILE I --
-- ROOK?

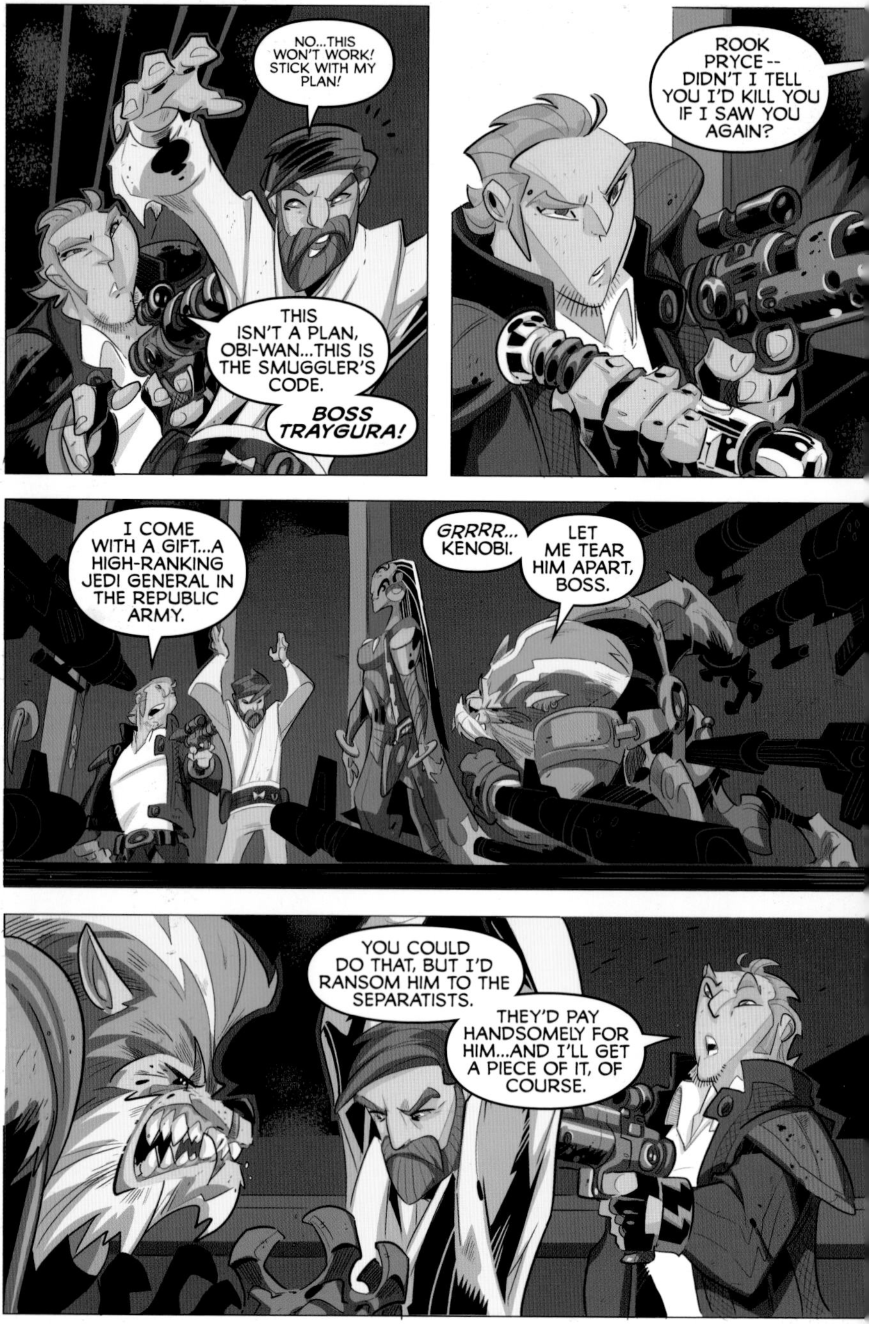

NO...THIS WON'T WORK! STICK WITH MY PLAN!
THIS ISN'T A PLAN, OBI-WAN...THIS IS THE SMUGGLER'S CODE.
BOSS TRAYGURA!
ROOK PRYCE -- DIDN'T I TELL YOU I'D KILL YOU IF I SAW YOU AGAIN?
I COME WITH A GIFT...A HIGH-RANKING JEDI GENERAL IN THE REPUBLIC ARMY.
GRRRR... KENOBI.
LET ME TEAR HIM APART, BOSS.
YOU COULD DO THAT, BUT I'D RANSOM HIM TO THE SEPARATISTS.
THEY'D PAY HANDSOMELY FOR HIM...AND I'LL GET A PIECE OF IT, OF COURSE.

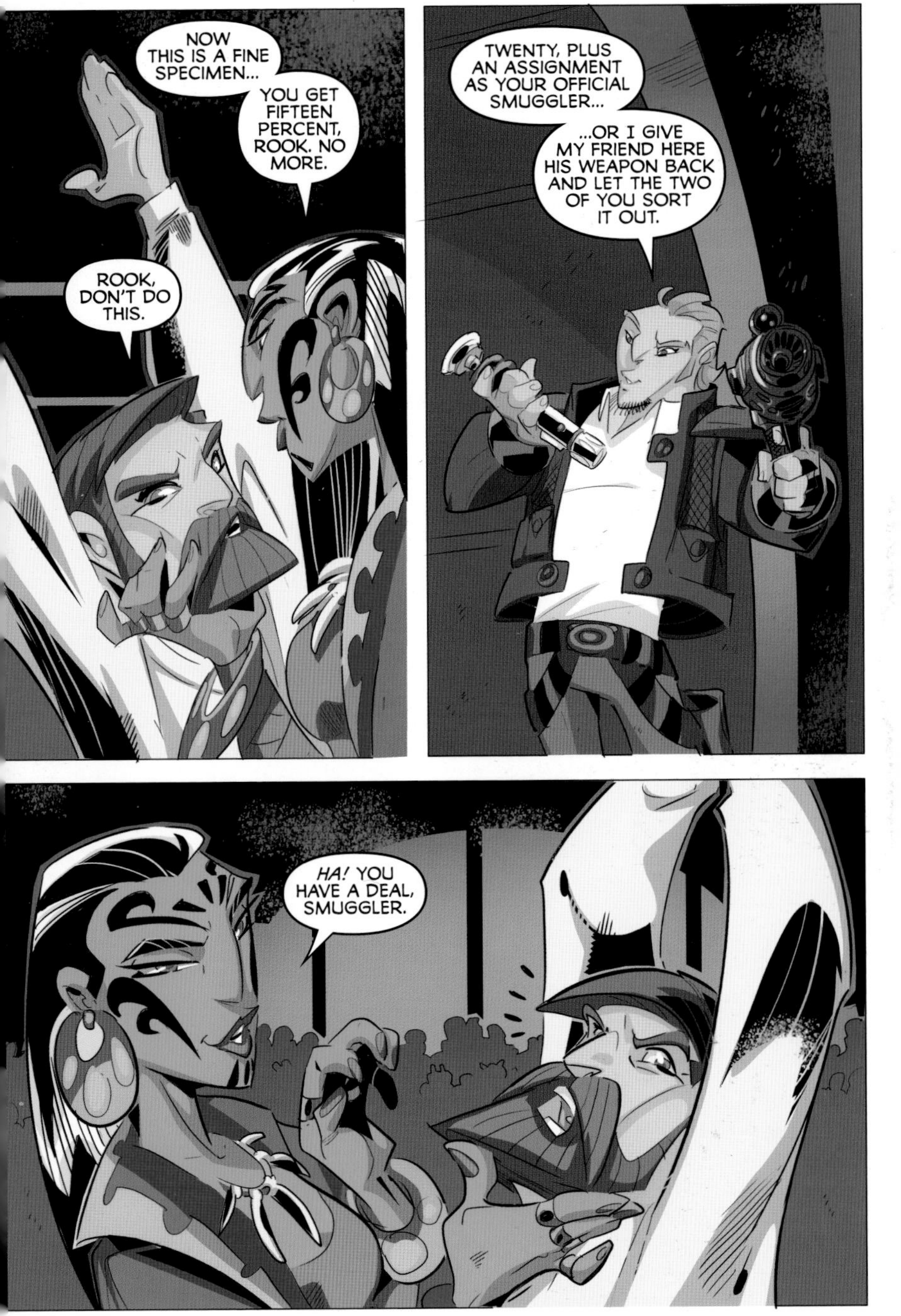
NOW THIS IS A FINE SPECIMEN...
YOU GET FIFTEEN PERCENT, ROOK. NO MORE.
ROOK, DON'T DO THIS.
TWENTY, PLUS AN ASSIGNMENT AS YOUR OFFICIAL SMUGGLER...
...OR I GIVE MY FRIEND HERE HIS WEAPON BACK AND LET THE TWO OF YOU SORT IT OUT.
HA! YOU HAVE A DEAL, SMUGGLER.

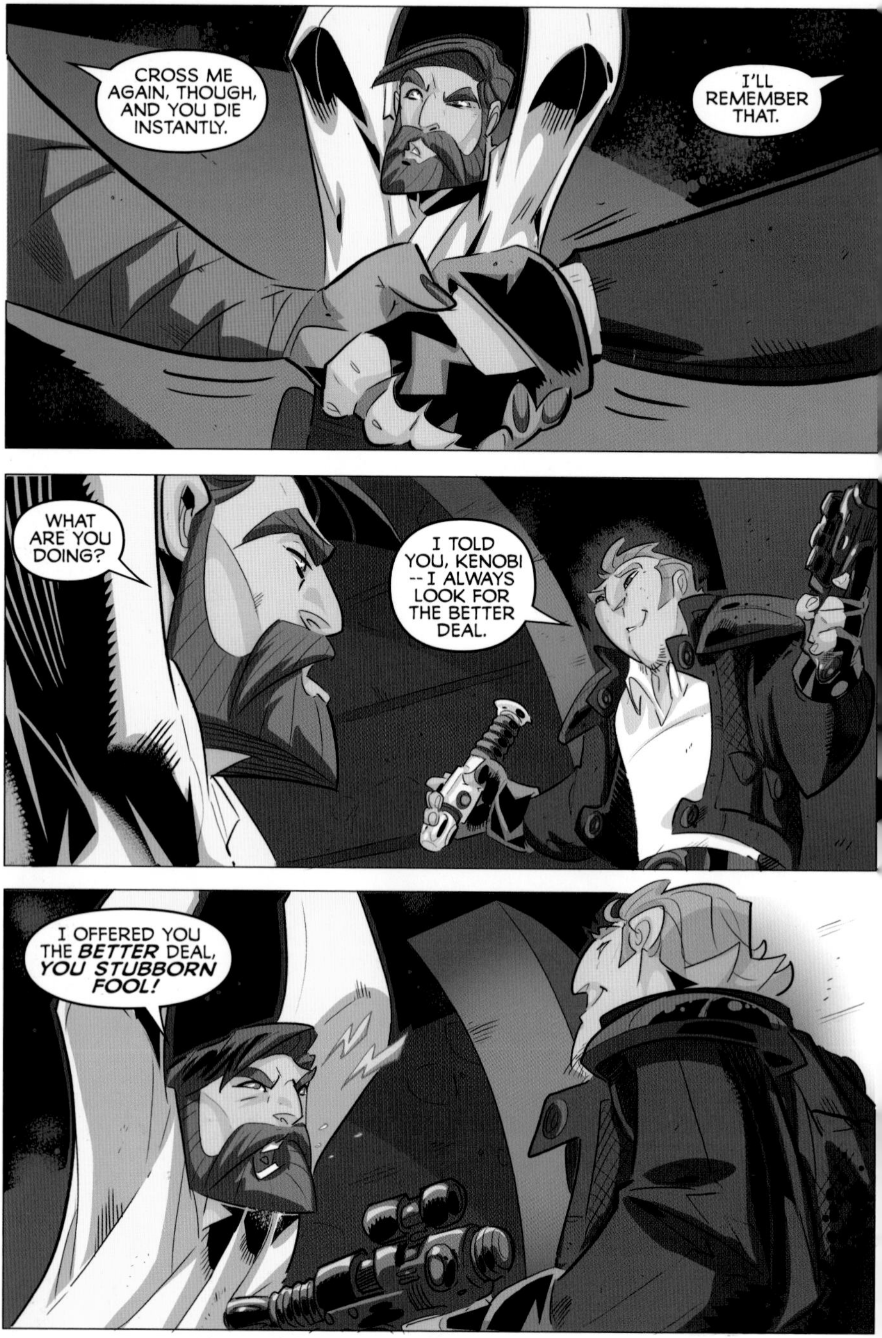
CROSS ME AGAIN, THOUGH, AND YOU DIE INSTANTLY.
I'LL REMEMBER THAT.
WHAT ARE YOU DOING?
I TOLD YOU, KENOBI -- I ALWAYS LOOK FOR THE BETTER DEAL.
I OFFERED YOU THE *BETTER* DEAL, ***YOU STUBBORN FOOL!***

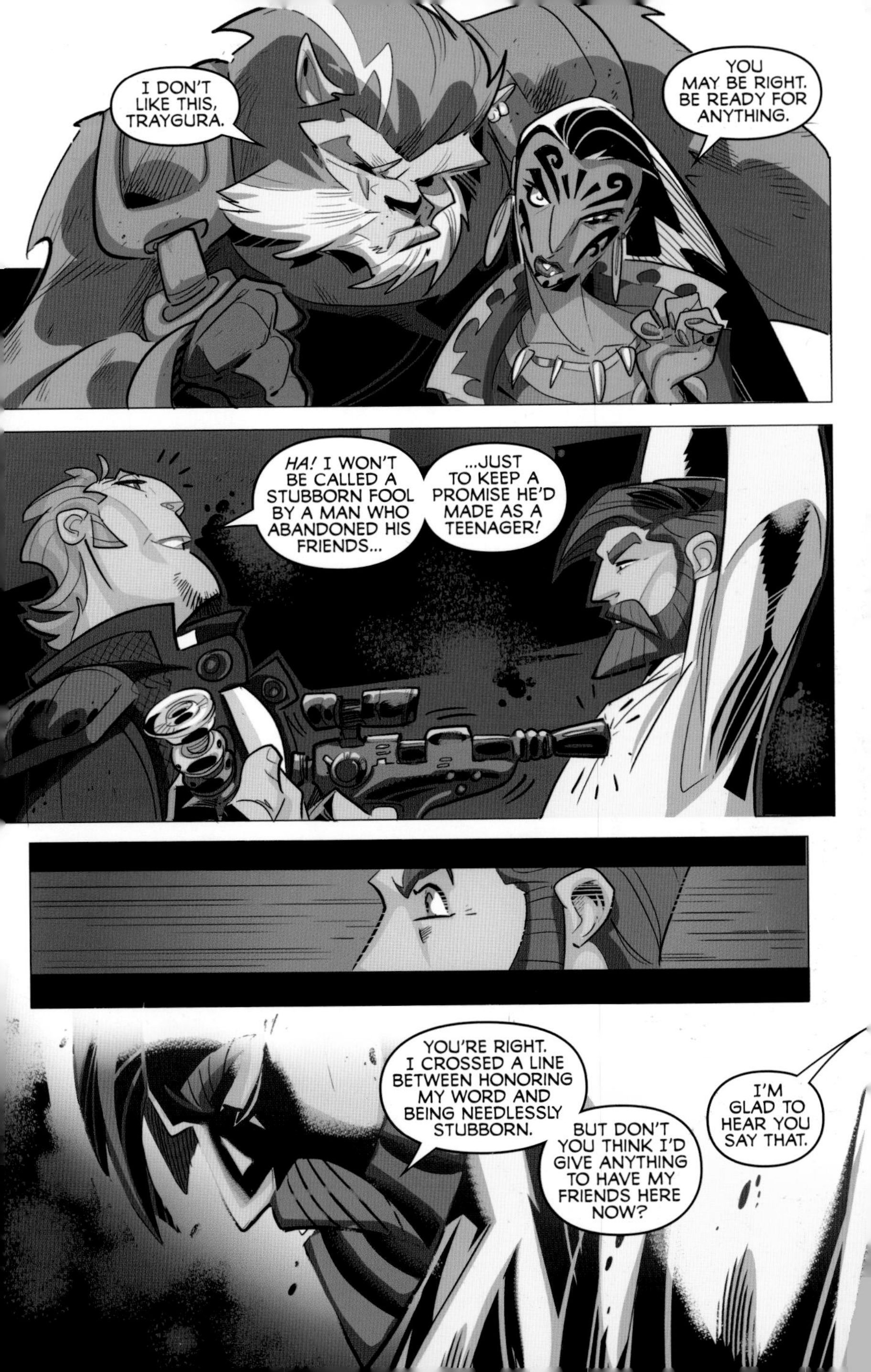
I DON'T LIKE THIS, TRAYGURA.
YOU MAY BE RIGHT. BE READY FOR ANYTHING.
HA! I WON'T BE CALLED A STUBBORN FOOL BY A MAN WHO ABANDONED HIS FRIENDS...
...JUST TO KEEP A PROMISE HE'D MADE AS A TEENAGER!
YOU'RE RIGHT. I CROSSED A LINE BETWEEN HONORING MY WORD AND BEING NEEDLESSLY STUBBORN.
BUT DON'T YOU THINK I'D GIVE ANYTHING TO HAVE MY FRIENDS HERE NOW?
I'M GLAD TO HEAR YOU SAY THAT.

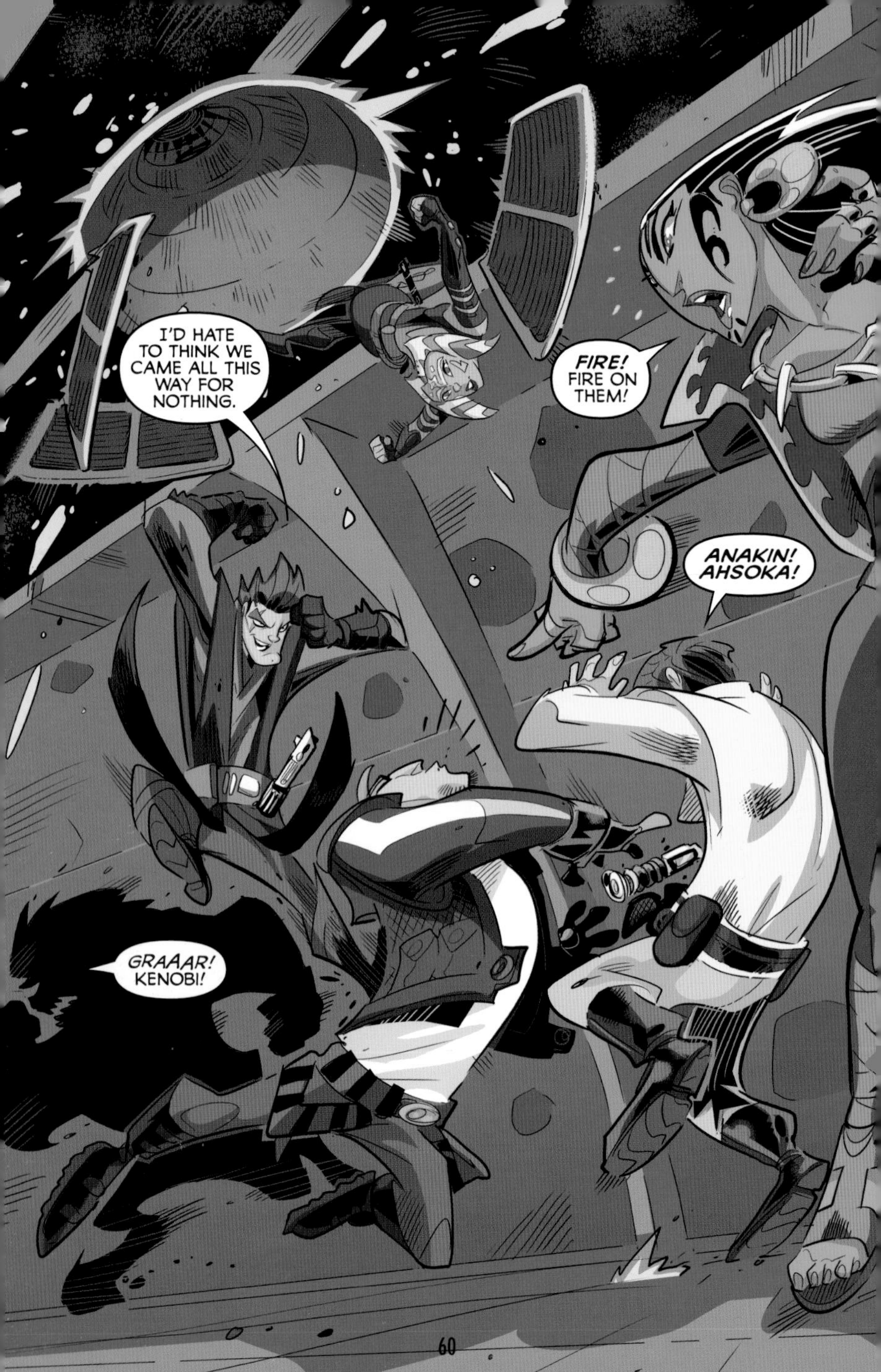
I'D HATE TO THINK WE CAME ALL THIS WAY FOR NOTHING.
FIRE! FIRE ON THEM!
ANAKIN! AHSOKA!
GRAAAR! KENOBI!

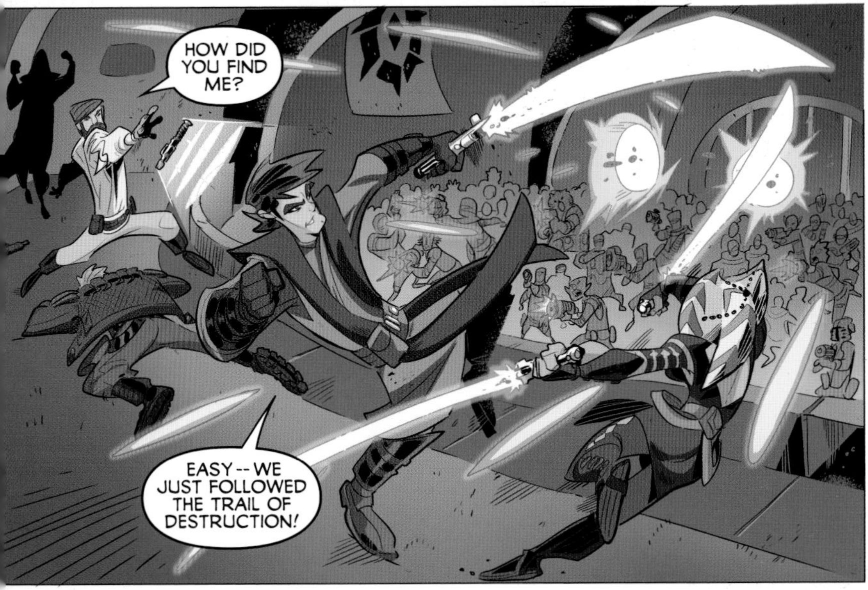
HOW DID YOU FIND ME?
EASY--WE JUST FOLLOWED THE TRAIL OF DESTRUCTION!

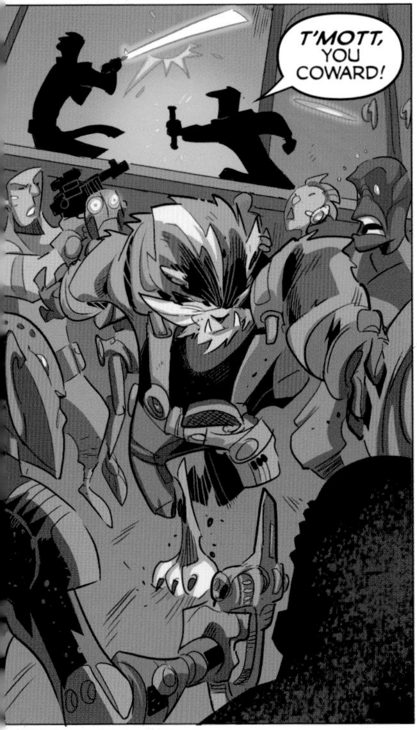
T'MOTT, YOU COWARD!

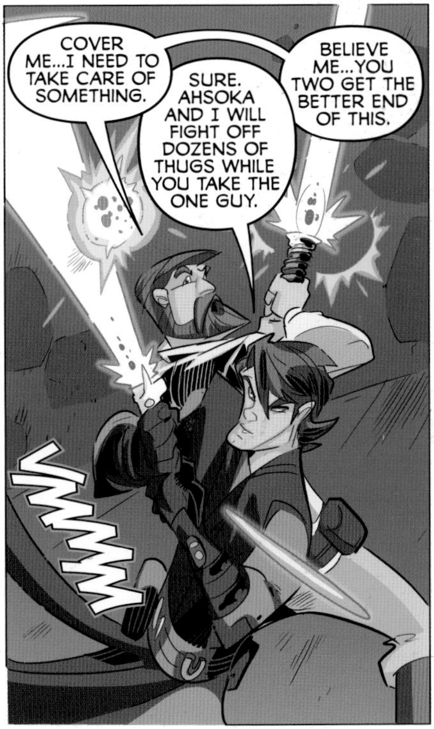
COVER ME...I NEED TO TAKE CARE OF SOMETHING.
SURE. AHSOKA AND I WILL FIGHT OFF DOZENS OF THUGS WHILE YOU TAKE THE ONE GUY.
BELIEVE ME...YOU TWO GET THE BETTER END OF THIS.
VWMMM

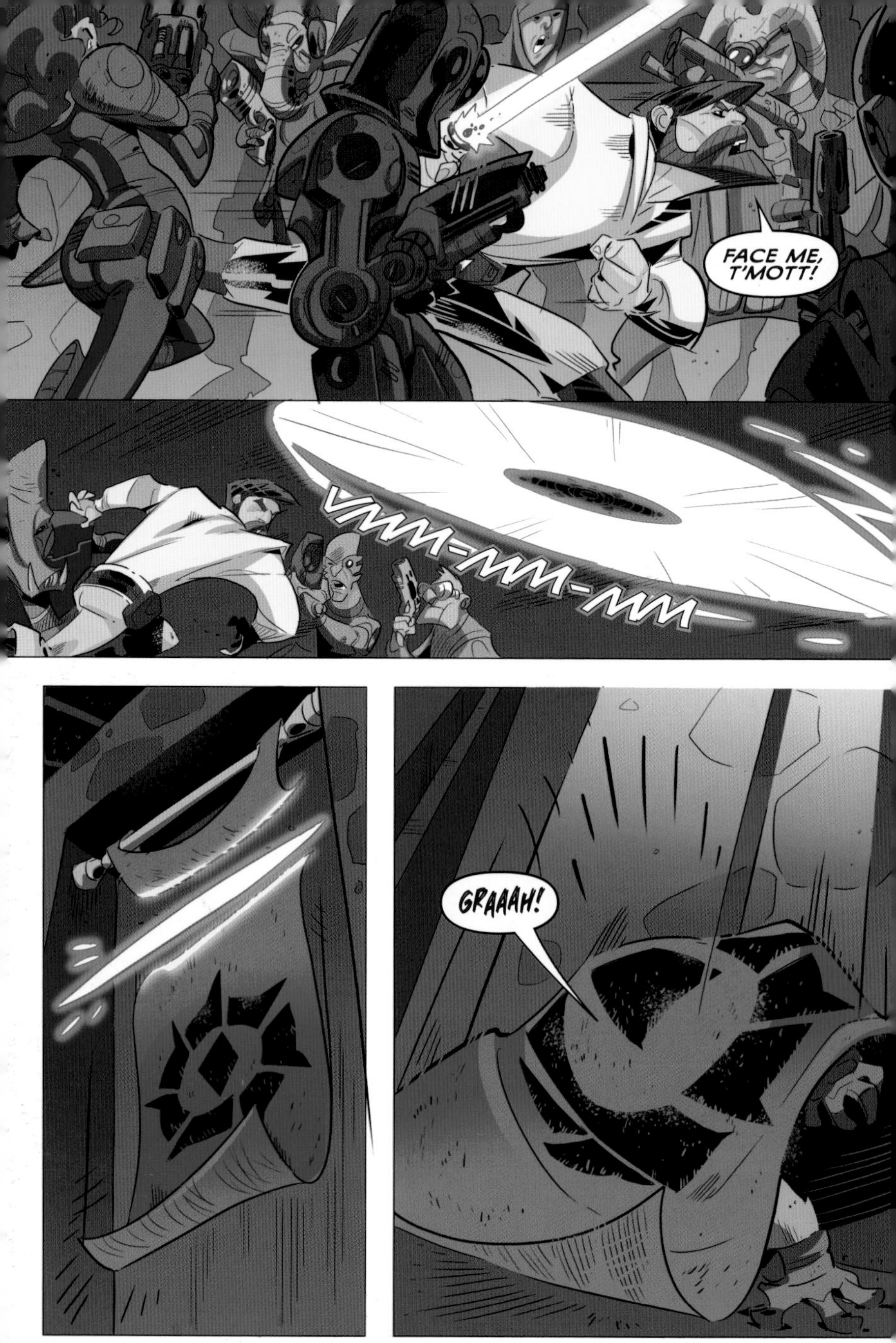
FACE ME, T'MOTT!
VMM-MM-MM
GRAAAH!

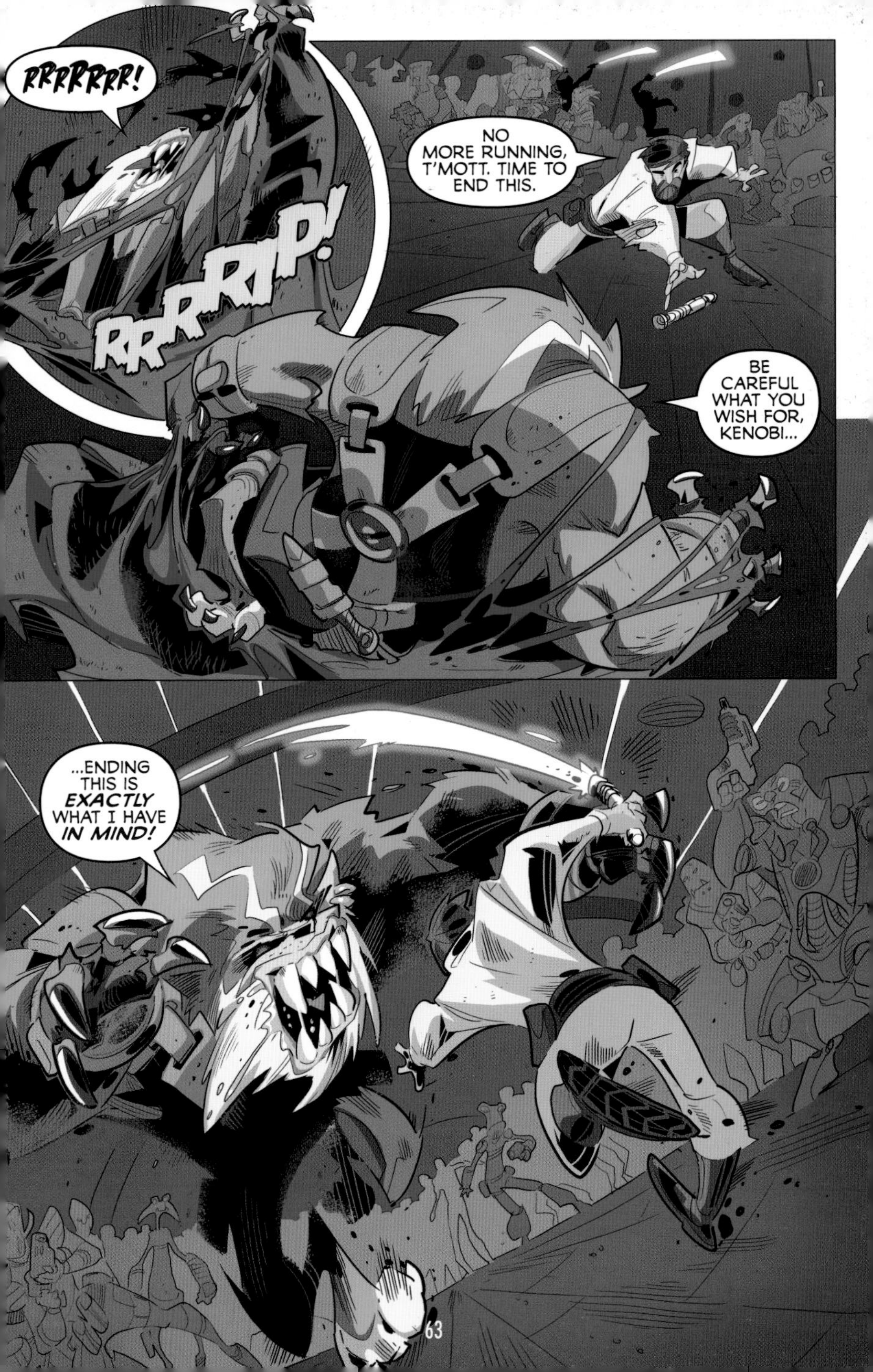
RRRRRRR!
NO MORE RUNNING, T'MOTT. TIME TO END THIS.
RRRRRIP!
BE CAREFUL WHAT YOU WISH FOR, KENOBI...
...ENDING THIS IS *EXACTLY* WHAT I HAVE *IN MIND!*

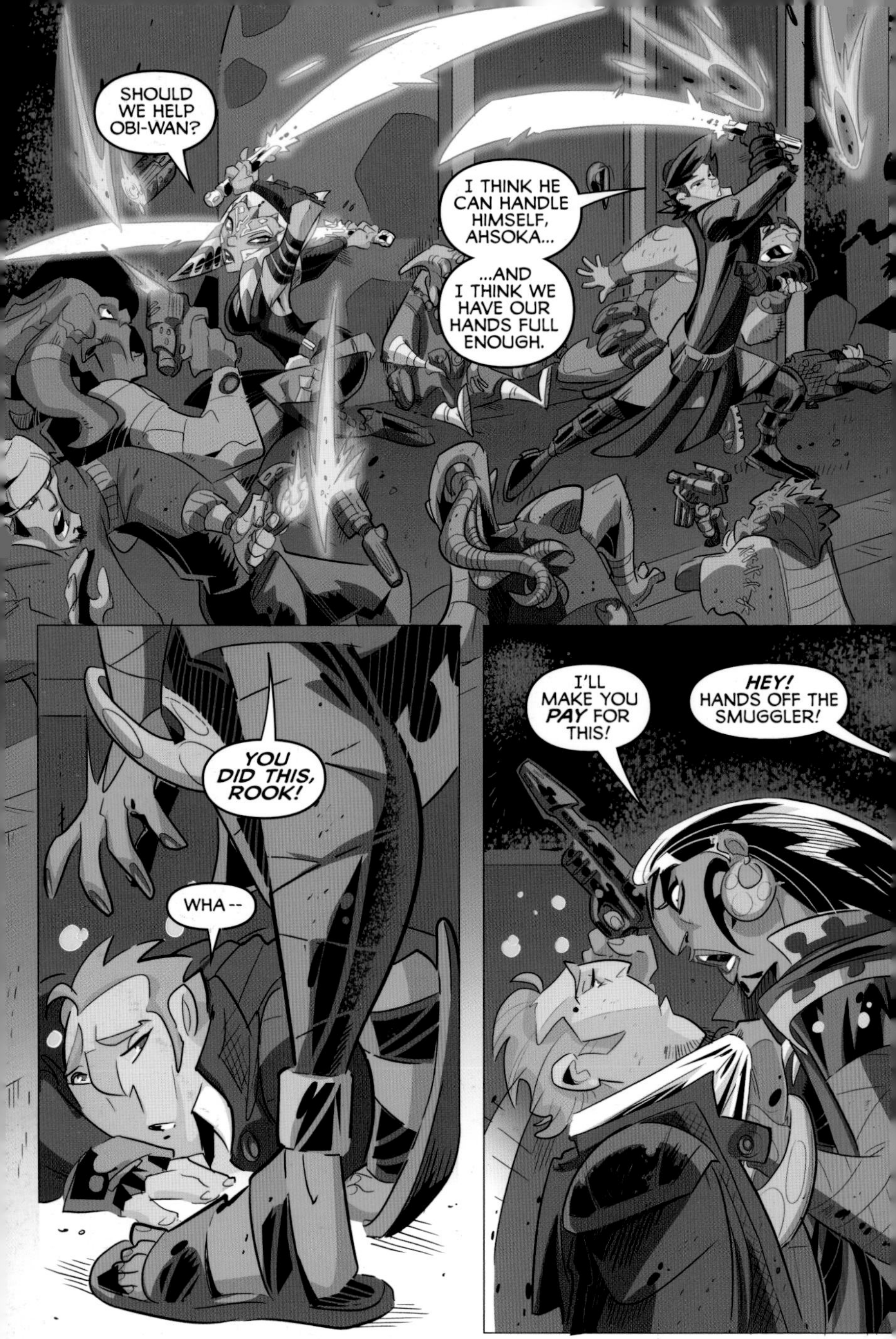
SHOULD WE HELP OBI-WAN?
I THINK HE CAN HANDLE HIMSELF, AHSOKA...
...AND I THINK WE HAVE OUR HANDS FULL ENOUGH.
YOU DID THIS, ROOK!
WHA --
I'LL MAKE YOU ***PAY*** FOR THIS!
HEY! HANDS OFF THE SMUGGLER!

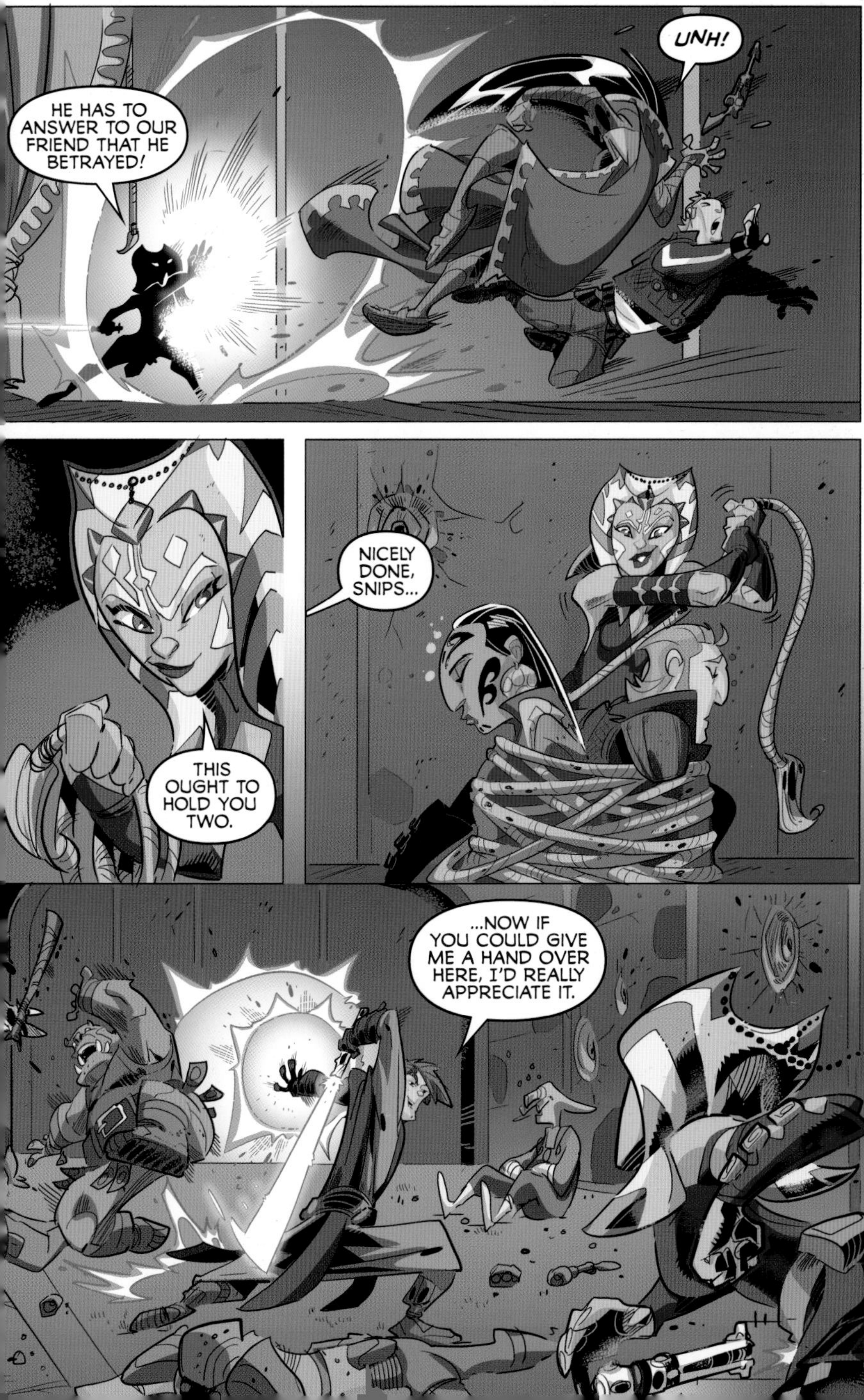
HE HAS TO ANSWER TO OUR FRIEND THAT HE BETRAYED!
UNH!
THIS OUGHT TO HOLD YOU TWO.
NICELY DONE, SNIPS...
...NOW IF YOU COULD GIVE ME A HAND OVER HERE, I'D REALLY APPRECIATE IT.

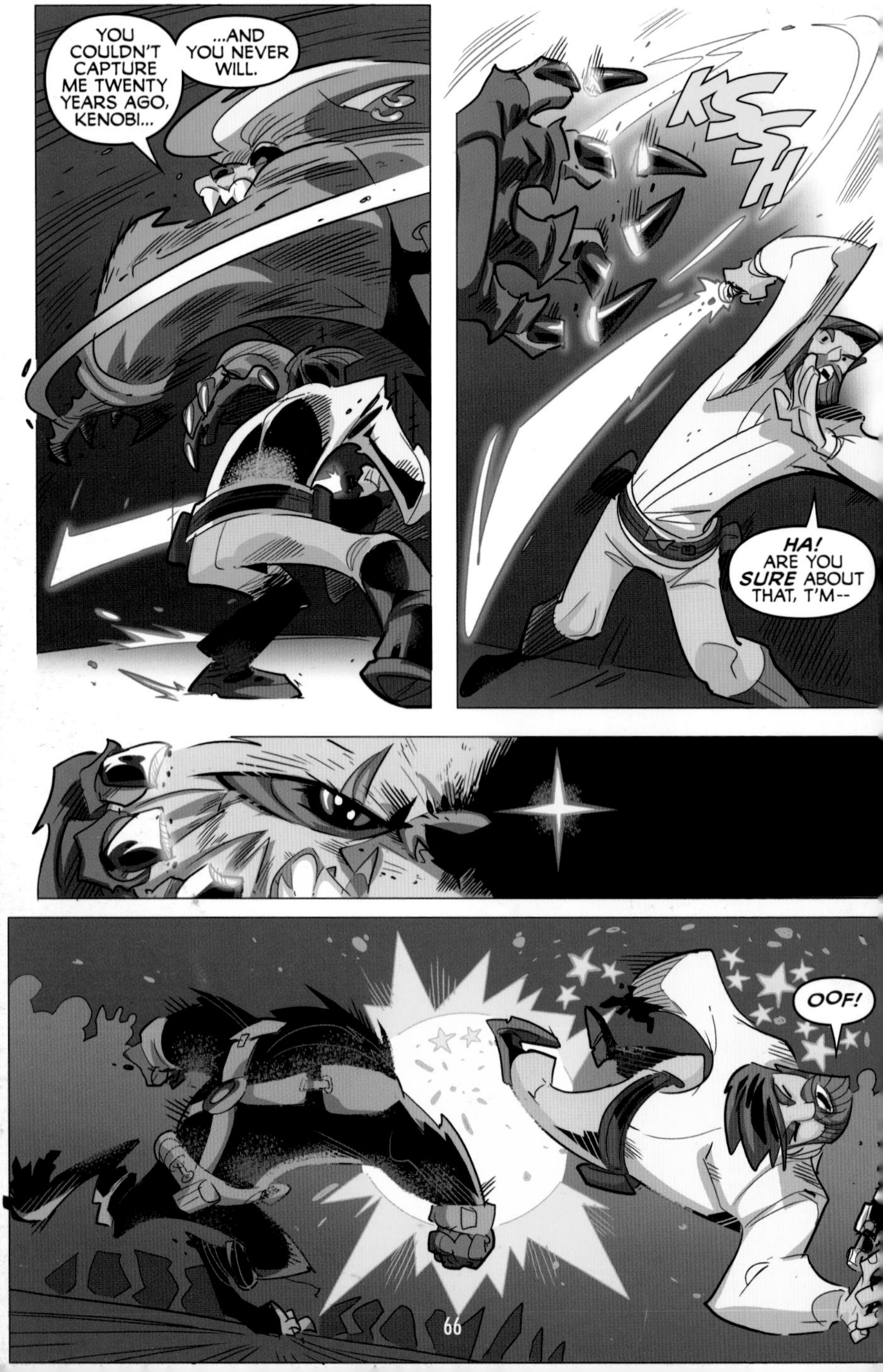

YOU COULDN'T CAPTURE ME TWENTY YEARS AGO, KENOBI...
...AND YOU NEVER WILL.
KSSH
HA! ARE YOU SURE ABOUT THAT, T'M--
OOF!

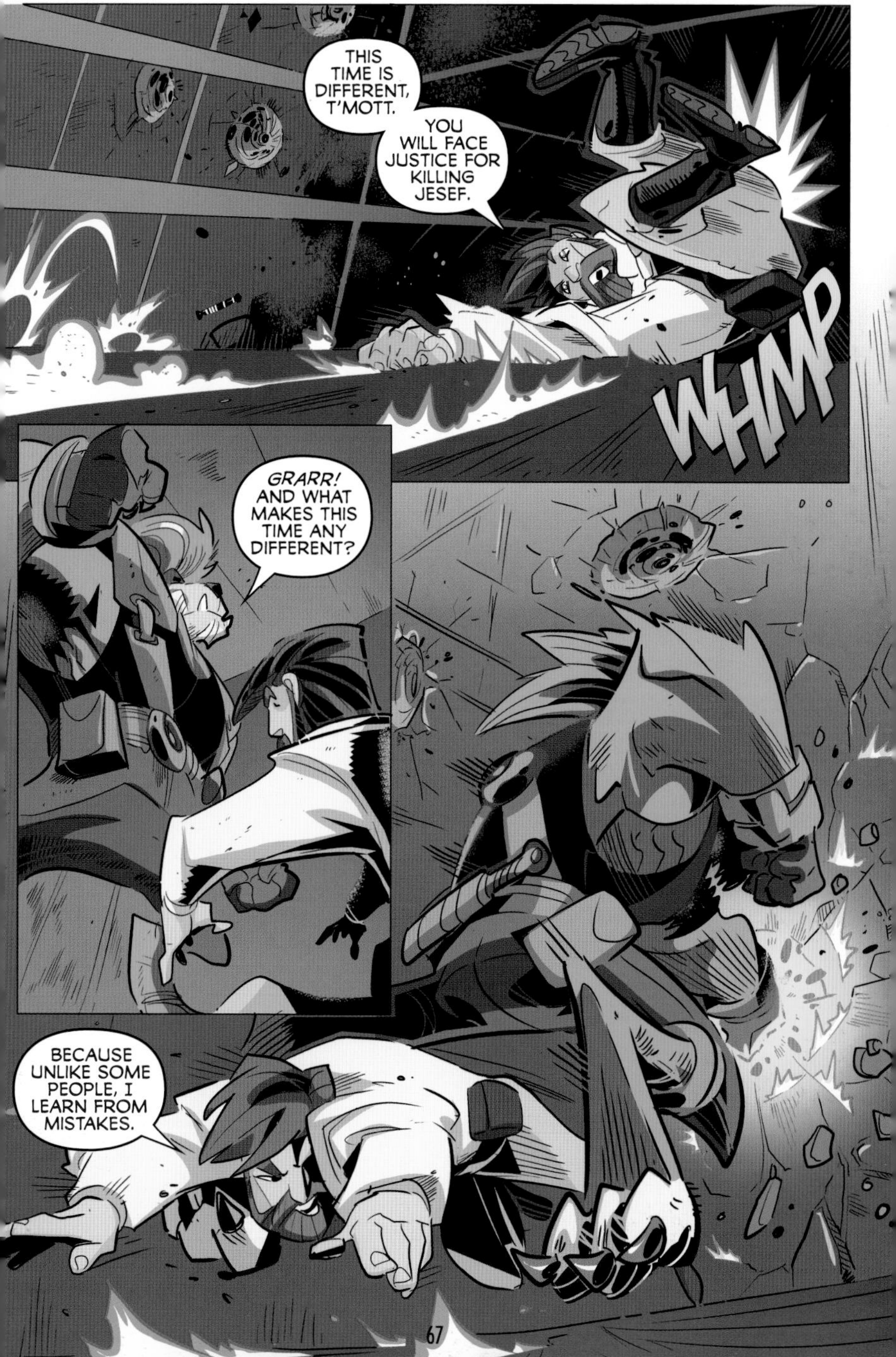
THIS TIME IS DIFFERENT, T'MOTT.
YOU WILL FACE JUSTICE FOR KILLING JESEF.
WHMP
GRARR! AND WHAT MAKES THIS TIME ANY DIFFERENT?
BECAUSE UNLIKE SOME PEOPLE, I LEARN FROM MISTAKES.

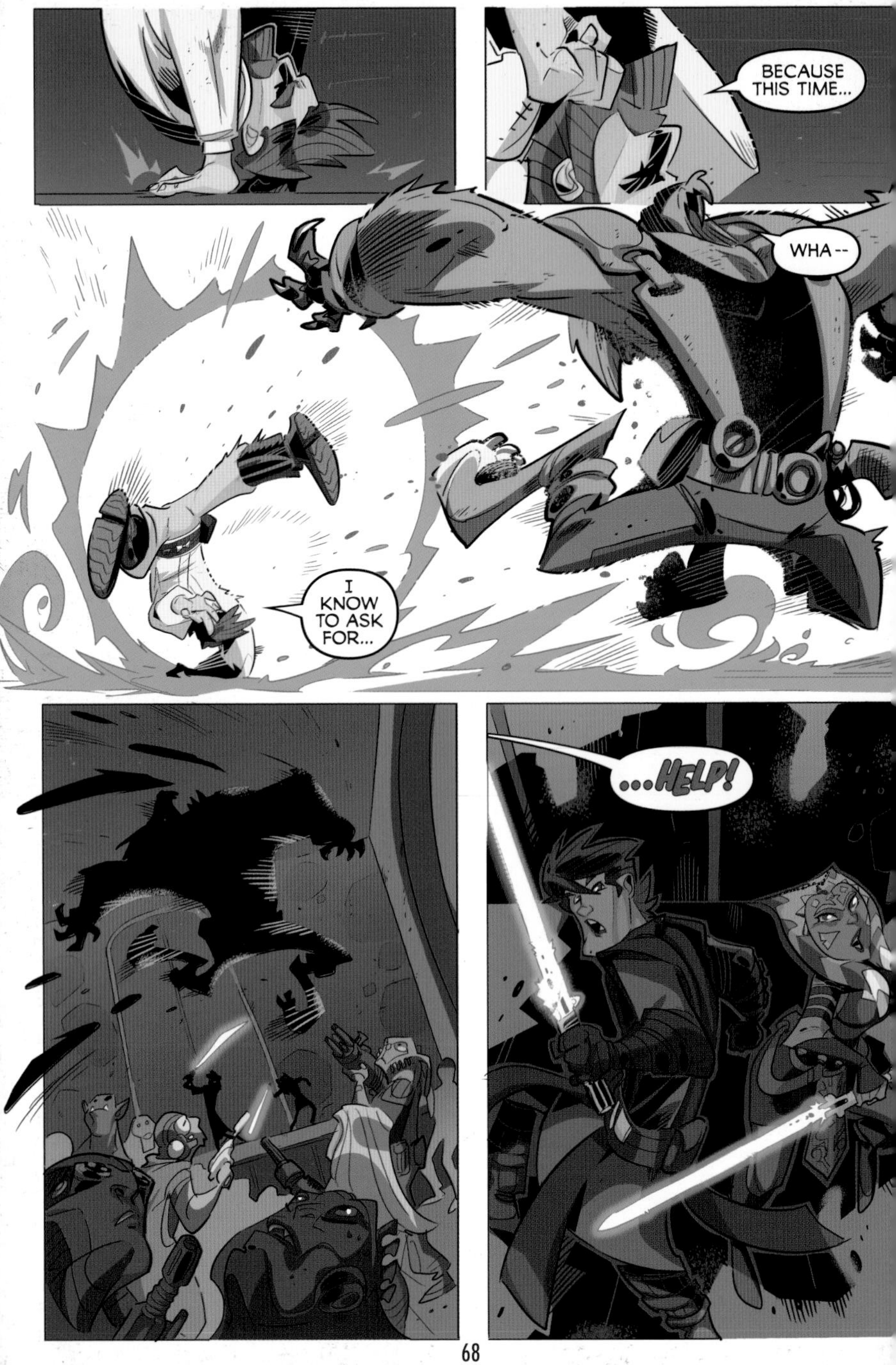
BECAUSE THIS TIME...
WHA--
I KNOW TO ASK FOR...
...HELP!

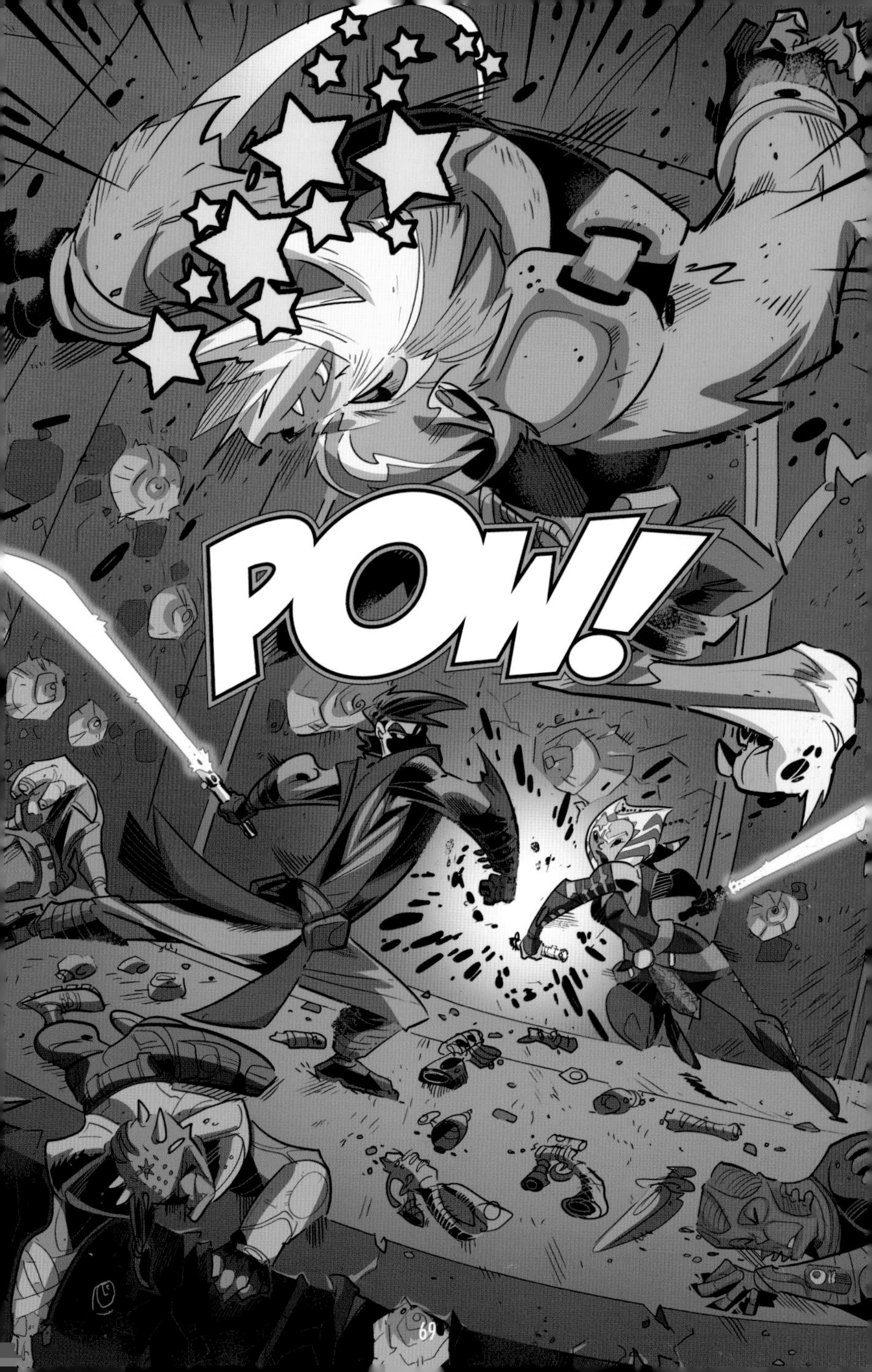
POW!

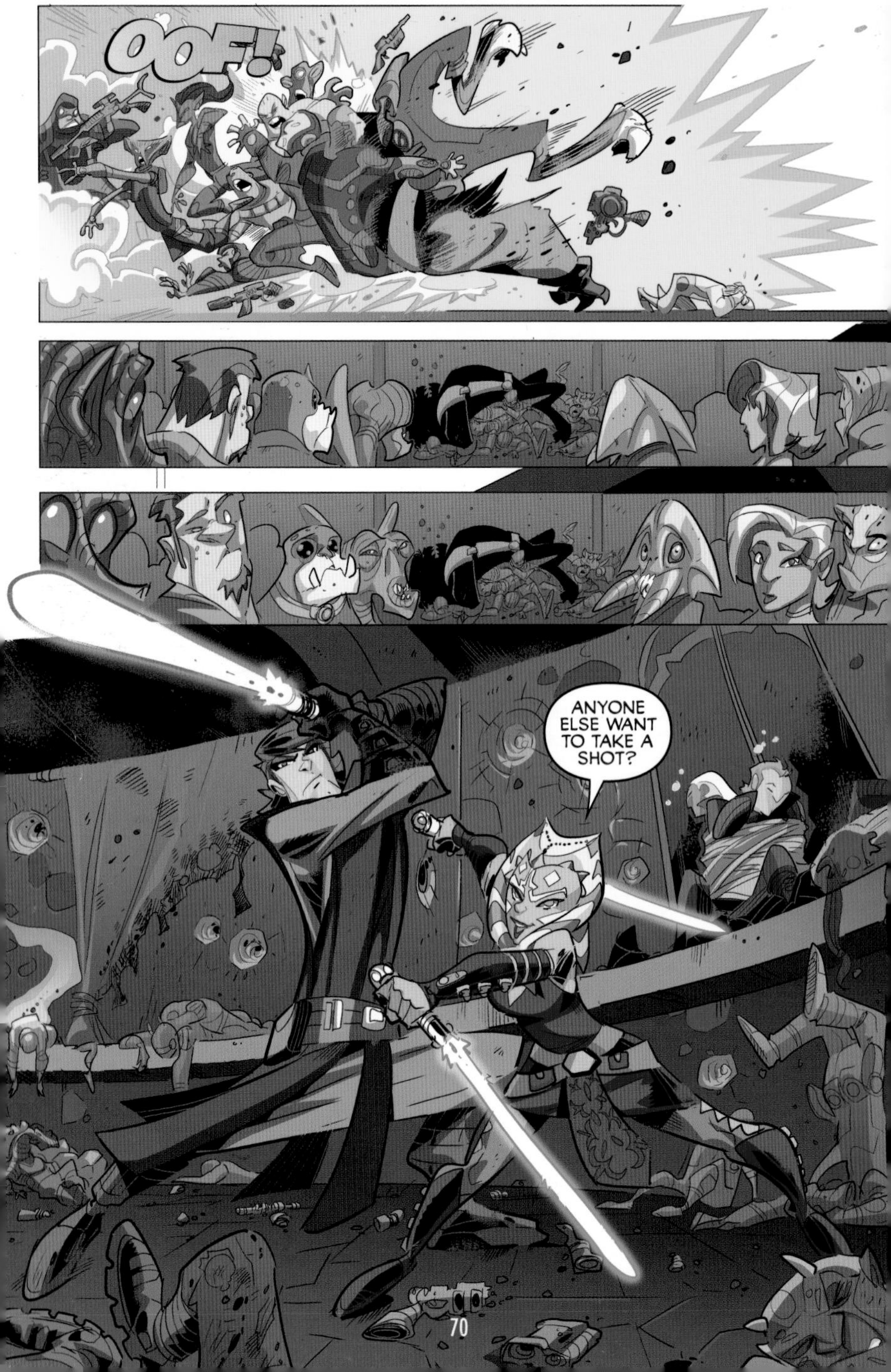
OOF!
ANYONE ELSE WANT TO TAKE A SHOT?

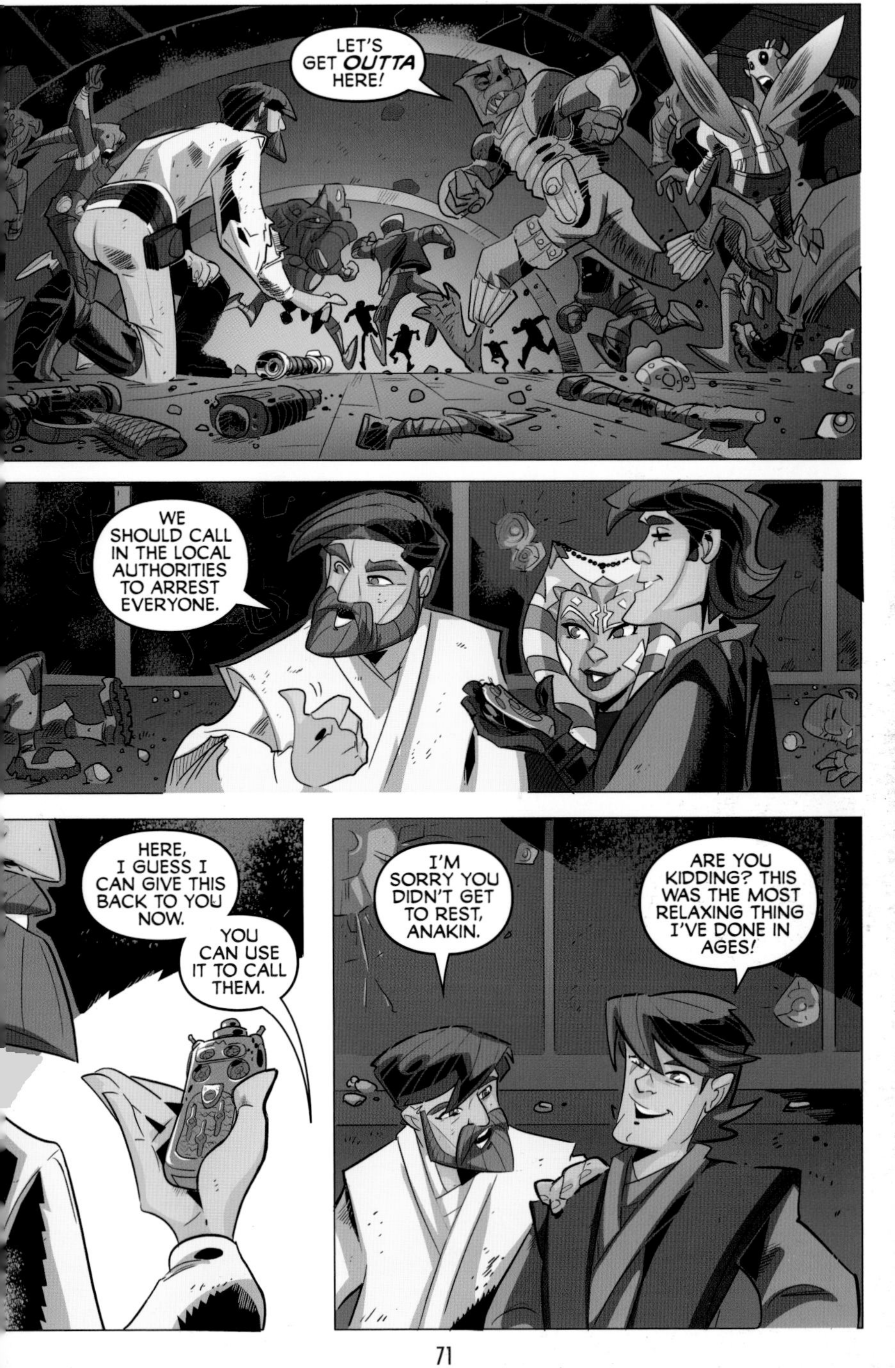
LET'S GET *OUTTA* HERE!
WE SHOULD CALL IN THE LOCAL AUTHORITIES TO ARREST EVERYONE.
HERE, I GUESS I CAN GIVE THIS BACK TO YOU NOW.
YOU CAN USE IT TO CALL THEM.
I'M SORRY YOU DIDN'T GET TO REST, ANAKIN.
ARE YOU KIDDING? THIS WAS THE MOST RELAXING THING I'VE DONE IN AGES!

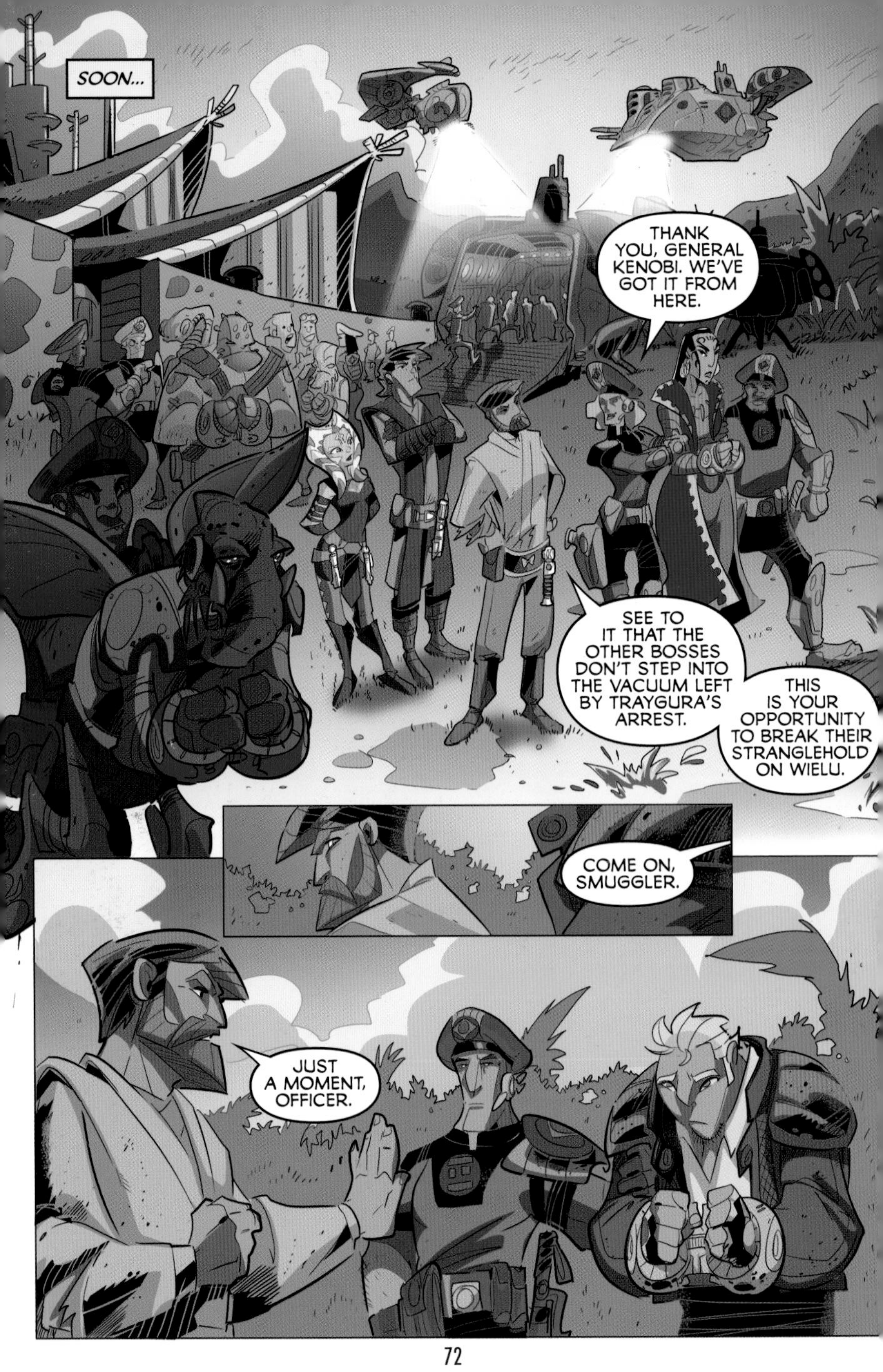
SOON...
THANK YOU, GENERAL KENOBI. WE'VE GOT IT FROM HERE.
SEE TO IT THAT THE OTHER BOSSES DON'T STEP INTO THE VACUUM LEFT BY TRAYGURA'S ARREST.
THIS IS YOUR OPPORTUNITY TO BREAK THEIR STRANGLEHOLD ON WIELU.
COME ON, SMUGGLER.
JUST A MOMENT, OFFICER.

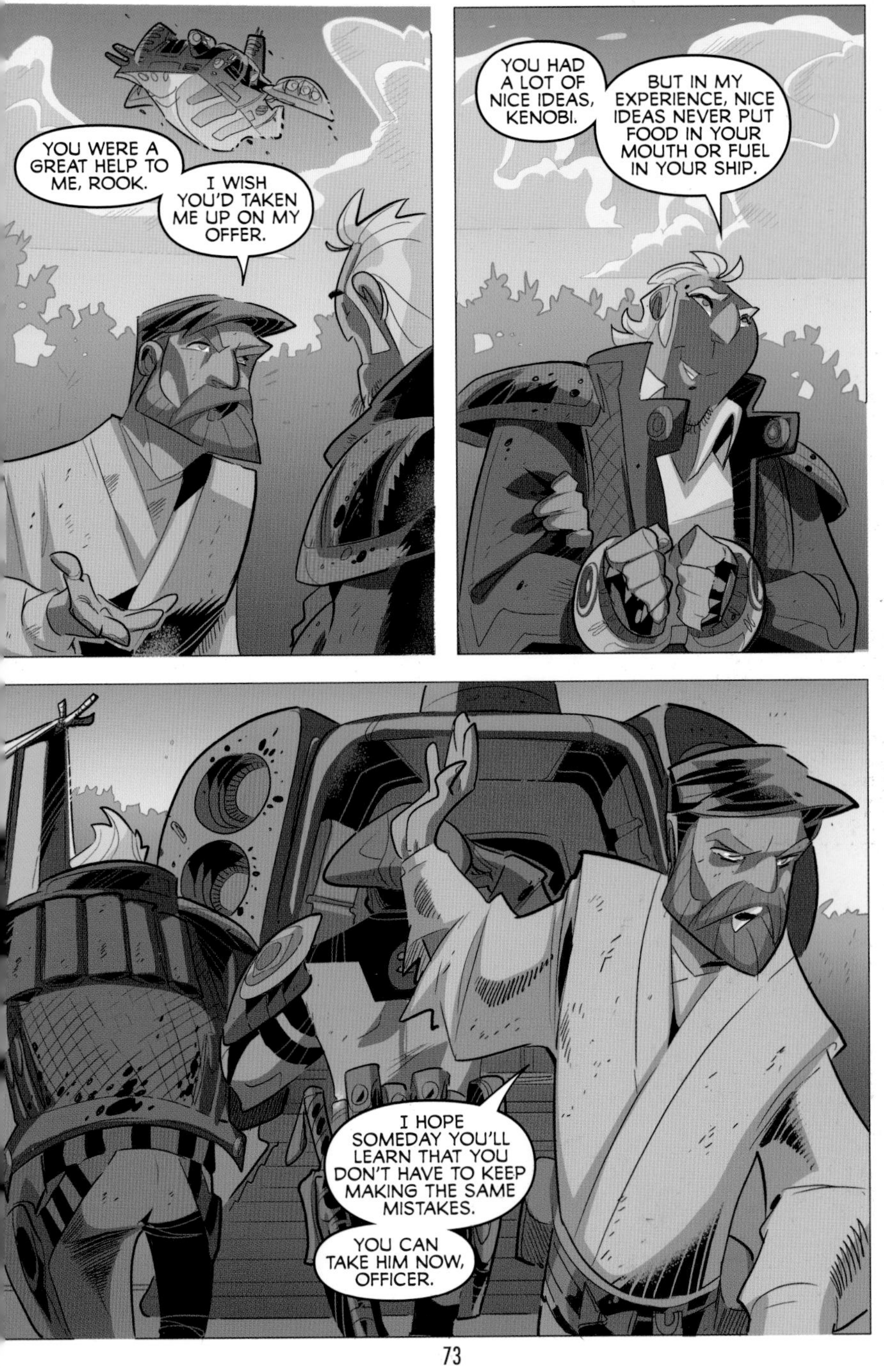
YOU WERE A GREAT HELP TO ME, ROOK.
I WISH YOU'D TAKEN ME UP ON MY OFFER.
YOU HAD A LOT OF NICE IDEAS, KENOBI.
BUT IN MY EXPERIENCE, NICE IDEAS NEVER PUT FOOD IN YOUR MOUTH OR FUEL IN YOUR SHIP.
I HOPE SOMEDAY YOU'LL LEARN THAT YOU DON'T HAVE TO KEEP MAKING THE SAME MISTAKES.
YOU CAN TAKE HIM NOW, OFFICER.

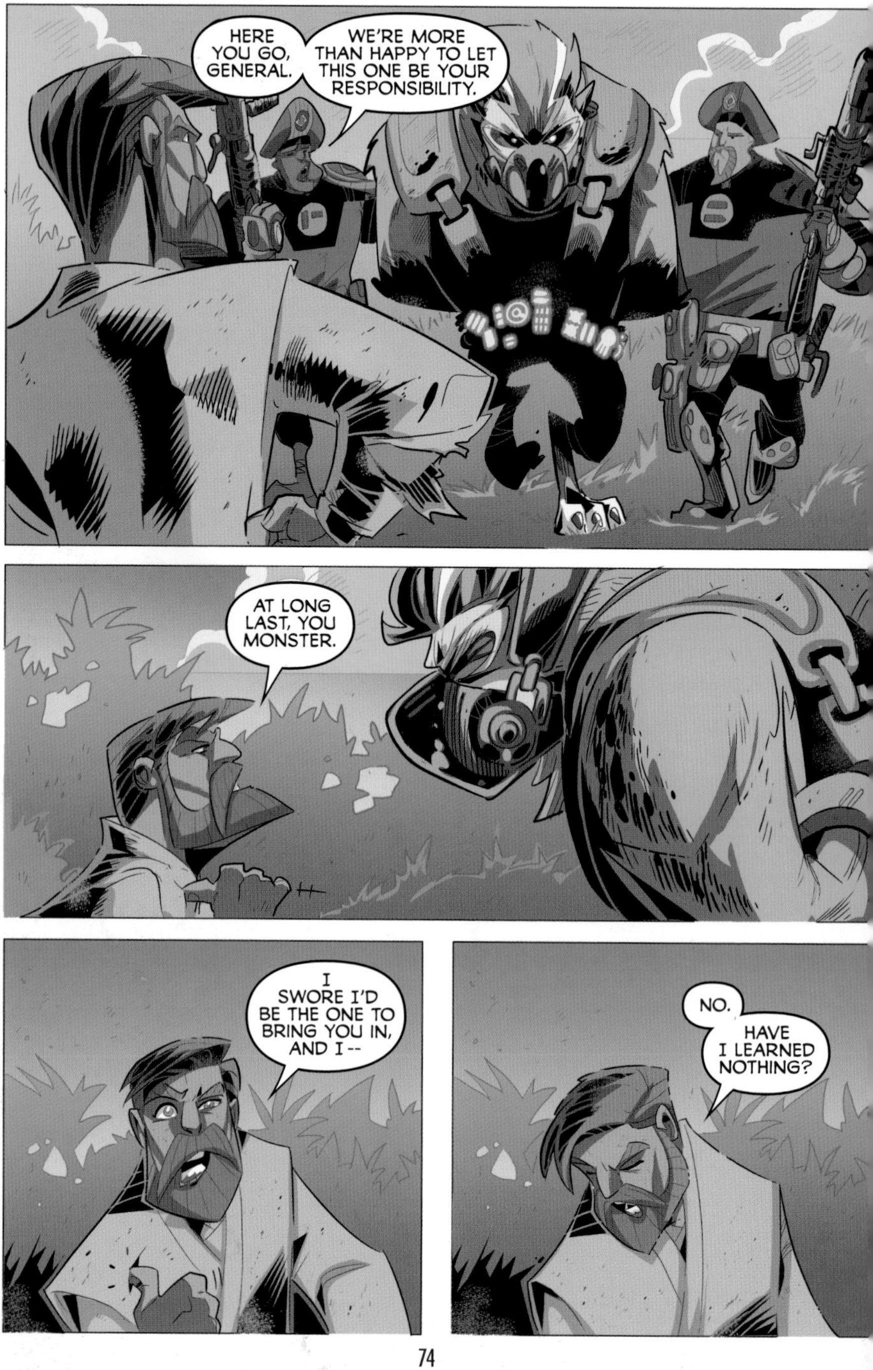
HERE YOU GO, GENERAL.
WE'RE MORE THAN HAPPY TO LET THIS ONE BE YOUR RESPONSIBILITY.
AT LONG LAST, YOU MONSTER.
I SWORE I'D BE THE ONE TO BRING YOU IN, AND I --
NO.
HAVE I LEARNED NOTHING?

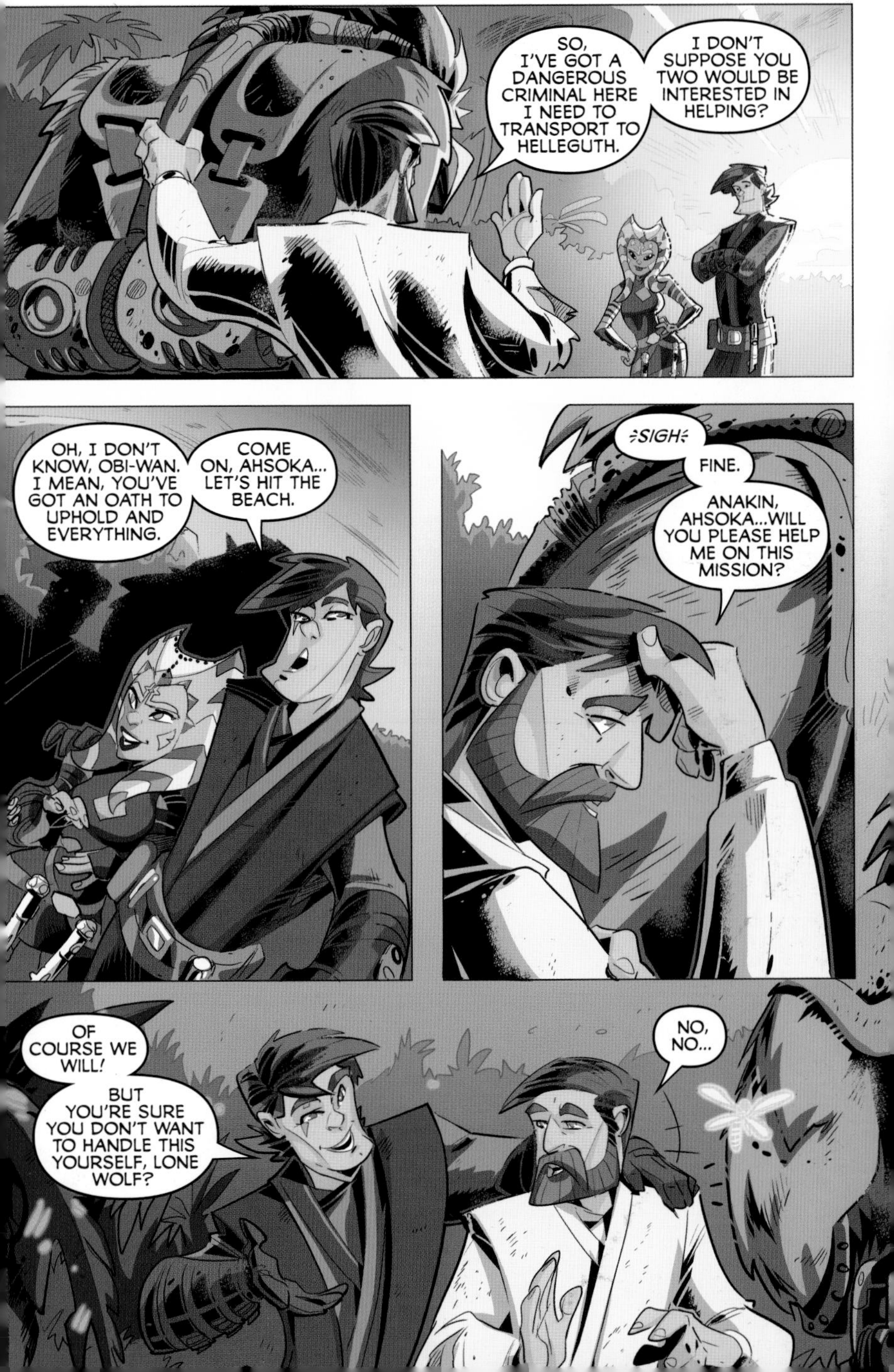
SO, I'VE GOT A DANGEROUS CRIMINAL HERE I NEED TO TRANSPORT TO HELLEGUTH.
I DON'T SUPPOSE YOU TWO WOULD BE INTERESTED IN HELPING?
OH, I DON'T KNOW, OBI-WAN. I MEAN, YOU'VE GOT AN OATH TO UPHOLD AND EVERYTHING.
COME ON, AHSOKA... LET'S HIT THE BEACH.
SIGH
FINE.
ANAKIN, AHSOKA...WILL YOU PLEASE HELP ME ON THIS MISSION?
OF COURSE WE WILL!
BUT YOU'RE SURE YOU DON'T WANT TO HANDLE THIS YOURSELF, LONE WOLF?
NO, NO...

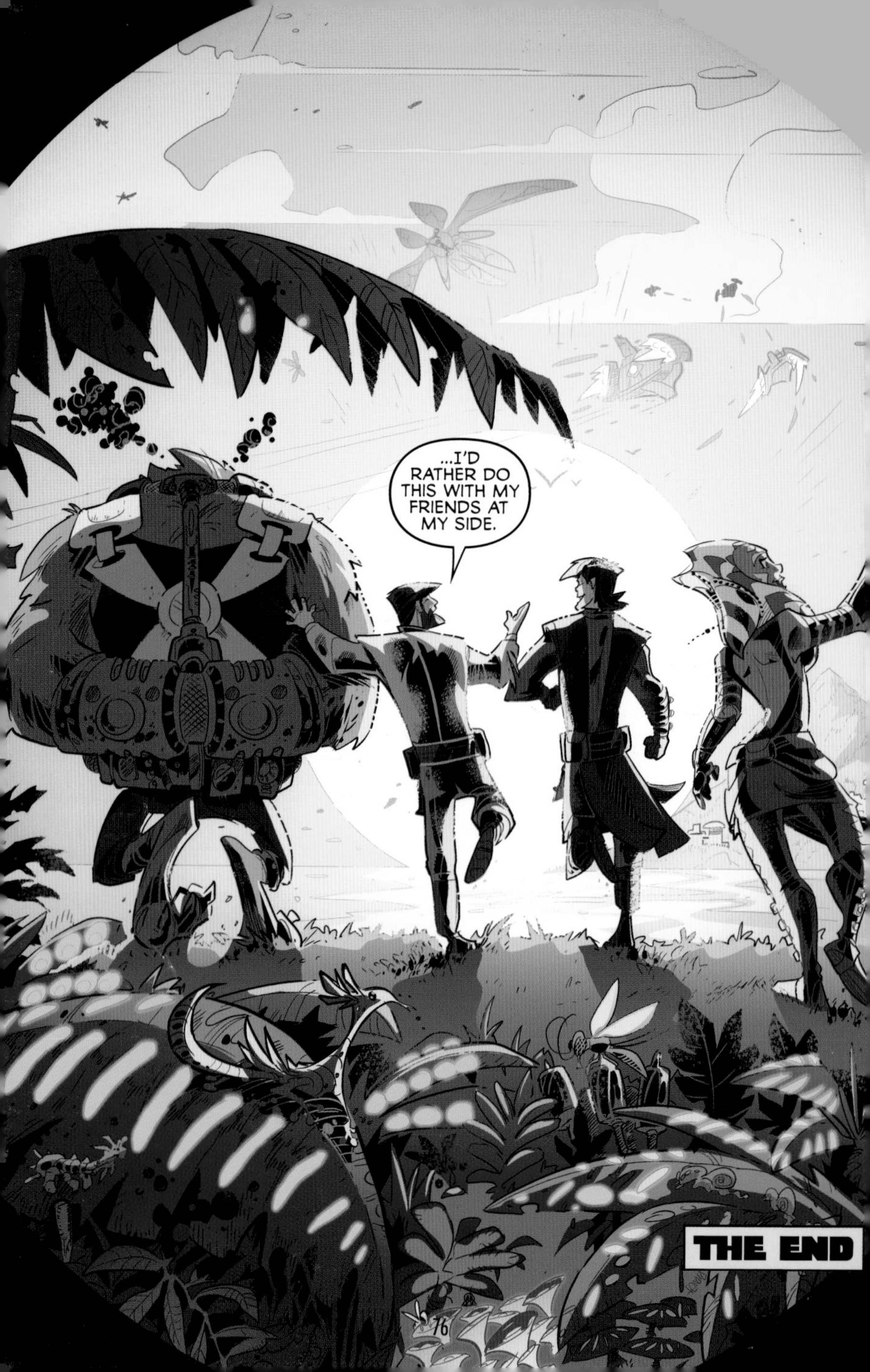
...I'D RATHER DO THIS WITH MY FRIENDS AT MY SIDE.
THE END

STAR WARS GRAPHIC NOVEL TIMELINE (IN YEARS)

Dawn of the Jedi—36,000 BSW4

Omnibus: Tales of the Jedi—5,000–3,986 BSW4

Knights of the Old Republic—3,964–3,963 BSW4

The Old Republic—3678, 3653, 3600 BSW4

Lost Tribe of the Sith—2974 BSW4

Knight Errant—1,032 BSW4

Jedi vs. Sith—1,000 BSW4

Jedi: The Dark Side—53 BSW4

Omnibus: Rise of the Sith—33 BSW4

Episode I: The Phantom Menace—32 BSW4

Omnibus: Emissaries and Assassins—32 BSW4

Omnibus: Quinlan Vos—Jedi in Darkness—31–30 BSW4

Omnibus: Menace Revealed—31–22 BSW4

Honor and Duty—22 BSW4

Blood Ties—22 BSW4

Episode II: Attack of the Clones—22 BSW4

Clone Wars—22–19 BSW4

Omnibus: Clone Wars—22–19 BSW4

Clone Wars Adventures—22–19 BSW4

Darth Maul: Death Sentence—20 BSW4

Episode III: Revenge of the Sith—19 BSW4

Purge—19 BSW4

Dark Times—19 BSW4

Omnibus: Droids—5.5 BSW4

Omnibus: Boba Fett—3 BSW4–10 ASW4

Agent of the Empire—3 BSW4

The Force Unleashed—2 BSW4

Omnibus: At War with the Empire—1 BSW4

Episode IV: A New Hope—SW4

Star Wars—0 ASW4

Classic Star Wars—0–3 ASW4

Omnibus: A Long Time Ago. . . .—0–4 ASW4

Empire—0 ASW4

Omnibus: The Other Sons of Tatooine—0 ASW4

Omnibus: Early Victories—0–3 ASW4

Jabba the Hutt: The Art of the Deal—1 ASW4

Episode V: The Empire Strikes Back—3 ASW4

Omnibus: Shadows of the Empire—3.5–4.5 ASW4

Episode VI: Return of the Jedi—4 ASW4

Omnibus: X-Wing Rogue Squadron—4–5 ASW4

The Thrawn Trilogy—9 ASW4

Dark Empire—10 ASW4

Crimson Empire—11 ASW4

Jedi Academy: Leviathan—12 ASW4

Union—19 ASW4

Chewbacca—25 ASW4

Invasion—25 ASW4

Legacy—130–138 ASW4

Dawn of the Jedi
36,000 years before
Star Wars: A New Hope

Old Republic Era
25,000–1000 years before
Star Wars: A New Hope

Rise of the Empire Era
1000–0 years before Star
Wars: A New Hope

Rebellion Era
0–5 years after
Star Wars: A New Hope

New Republic Era
5–25 years after
Star Wars: A New Hope

New Jedi Order Era
25+ years after
Star Wars: A New Hope

Legacy Era
130+ years after
Star Wars: A New Hope

Vector
Crosses four eras in timeline

Volume 1 contains:
Knights of the Old Republic Volume 5
Dark Times Volume 3
Volume 2 contains:
Rebellion Volume 4
Legacy Volume 6

Infinities
Does not apply to timeline

Sergio Aragones Stomps Star Wars
Star Wars Tales
Omnibus: Infinities
Tag and Bink
Star Wars Visionaries

BSW4 = before *Episode IV: A New Hope.* ASW4 = after *Episode IV: A New Hope.*

FOR MORE ADVENTURE IN A GALAXY FAR, FAR, AWAY . . .

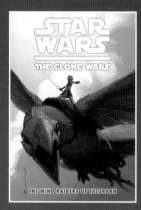

STAR WARS
THE CLONE WARS
THE WIND RAIDERS OF TALORAAN

STAR WARS: THE CLONE WARS—THE WIND RAIDERS OF TALORAAN
978-1-59582-231-4 | $7.99

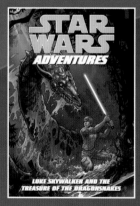

STAR WARS
ADVENTURES
LUKE SKYWALKER AND THE
TREASURE OF THE DRAGONSNAKES

STAR WARS ADVENTURES: LUKE SKYWALKER AND THE TREASURE OF THE DRAGONSNAKES
978-1-59582-347-2 | $7.99

STAR WARS ADVENTURES: HAN SOLO AND THE HOLLOW MOON OF KHORYA
978-1-59582-198-0 | $7.99

STAR WARS ADVENTURES: PRINCESS LEIA AND THE ROYAL RANSOM
978-1-59582-147-8 | $7.99

STAR WARS ADVENTURES: THE WILL OF DARTH VADER
978-1-59582-435-6 | $7.99

STAR WARS ADVENTURES: BOBA FETT AND THE SHIP OF FEAR
978-1-59582-436-3 | $7.99

STAR WARS: THE CLONE WARS—SHIPYARDS OF DOOM
978-1-59582-207-9 | $7.99

STAR WARS: THE CLONE WARS—CRASH COURSE
978-1-59582-230-7 | $7.99

STAR WARS: THE CLONE WARS—SLAVES OF THE REPUBLIC
978-1-59582-349-6 | $9.99

STAR WARS: THE CLONE WARS—THE COLOSSUS OF DESTINY
978-1-59582-416-5 | $7.99

STAR WARS: THE CLONE WARS—IN SERVICE OF THE REPUBLIC
978-1-59582-487-5 | $7.99

STAR WARS: THE CLONE WARS—HERO OF THE CONFEDERACY
978-1-59582-552-0 | $7.99

STAR WARS: THE CLONE WARS—DEADLY HANDS OF SHON-JU
978-1-59582-545-2 | $7.99

STAR WARS: THE CLONE WARS—THE ENEMY WITHIN
978-1-59582-845-3 | $7.99

STAR WARS: THE CLONE WARS—THE SITH HUNTERS
978-1-59582-949-8 | $7.99

STAR WARS: THE CLONE WARS—DEFENDERS OF THE LOST TEMPLE
978-1-61655-058-5 | $7.99

DARK HORSE BOOKS
darkhorse.com

AVAILABLE AT YOUR LOCAL COMICS SHOP OR BOOKSTORE

To find a comics shop in your area, call 1-888-266-4226
For more information or to order direct: • On the web: darkhorse.com • E-mail: mailorder@darkhorse.com
Phone: 1-800-862-0052 Mon.–Fri. 9 AM to 5 PM Pacific Time.

STAR WARS ®

CLONE WARS
ADVENTURES

Don't miss any of the action-packed adventures of your favorite **STAR WARS**® characters, available at comics shops and bookstores in a galaxy near you!

$6.99 each!

Volume 1	**Volume 2**	**Volume 3**	**Volume 4**	**Volume 5**
ISBN 978-1-59307-243-8	ISBN 978-1-59307-271-1	ISBN 978-1-59307-307-7	ISBN 978-1-59307-402-9	ISBN 978-1-59307-483-8

Volume 6	**Volume 7**	**Volume 8**	**Volume 9**	**Volume 10**
ISBN 978-1-59307-567-5	ISBN 978-1-59307-678-8	ISBN 978-1-59307-680-1	ISBN 978-1-59307-832-4	ISBN 978-1-59307-878-2